Not Just Pretty B

Making Talismans gives readers the practical tech.
turning mundane objects into living entities of power that will bring about real change in their lives.

By pooling techniques from areas as diverse as Shamanism, Paganism, the Esoteric Order of the Golden Dawn, and Dion Fortune, *Making Talismans* provides training in magical techniques from the simplest to the most complex. With these instructions, even inexperienced practitioners will become capable of performing advanced magical talismanic operations.

Making Talismans provides practical methods for contacting the gods and angels who will breathe life into a talisman. It designates the correct colors, shapes, and names of power that should be used. It also contains previously unpublished information on testing whether a talisman is working, and the corrected versions of the magical signatures that will create a connection to the power of the planets. It even includes instructions on how to use the Earth to form a powerful natural talisman.

About the Author

Nick Farrell (United Kingdom) is an initiate of the Esoteric Order of the Golden Dawn and one of its branch orders, the Order of the Table Round. A former member of the Builders of the Adytum (BOTA) and the Servants of the Light (SOL), he heads a magical temple and conducts lectures throughout the world.

To Write to the Author

If you wish to contact the author or would like more information about this book, please write to the author in care of Llewellyn Worldwide and we will forward your request. Both the author and publisher appreciate hearing from you and learning of your enjoyment of this book and how it has helped you. Llewellyn Worldwide cannot guarantee that every letter written to the author can be answered, but all will be forwarded. Please write to:

Nick Farrell
℅ Llewellyn Worldwide
P.O. Box 64383, Dept. 0-7387-0004-5
St. Paul, MN 55164-0383, U.S.A.
Please enclose a self-addressed stamped envelope for reply,
or $1.00 to cover costs. If outside U.S.A., enclose
international postal reply coupon.

Many of Llewellyn's authors have websites with additional information and resources. For more information, please visit our website at
http://www.llewellyn.com

For Llewellyn's free full-color catalog,
write to *New Worlds* at the above address,
or call 1-800 THE MOON.

MAKING
Talismans

Living Entities of Power

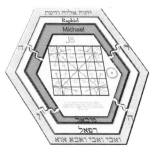

A Complete Magical System to Bring About Inner & Outer Change

Nick Farrell

2001
Llewellyn Publications
St. Paul, Minnesota 55164-0383, U.S.A.

First Edition
First Printing, 2001

Book design by Donna Burch
Cover art © 2001 by Nick Farrell
Cover design by Gavin Dayton Duffy

The interview with Professor Ronald Hutton in chapter 2 is used by permission.

Library of Congress Cataloging-in-Publication Data
Farrell, Nick, 1965–
    Making talismans : living entities of power : a complete magical system to bring about inner & outer change / Nick Farrell.—1st ed.
        p. cm.
    Includes bibliographical references (p.) and index.
    ISBN 0-7387-0004-5
        1. Talismans. I. Title

BF1561 .F38 2001
133.4'4—dc21   2001029235

Llewellyn Publications
A Division of Llewellyn Worldwide, Ltd.
P.O. Box 64383, Dept. 0-7387-0004-5
St. Paul, MN 55164-0383, U.S.A.
www.llewellyn.com

 Printed in the United States of America on recycled paper

To Chic and Tabatha Cicero
who helped me when I was lost.

And to those other teachers,
seen and unseen,
who have assisted in my development.

Contents

Figures and Tables

Preface

My first magical experiment was an attempt to create a wealth talisman. I was seventeen years old and had read a handful of books on ceremonial magic and believed I had all the knowledge necessary to create a talisman. My principal grimoire was a tiny pamphlet, long since discarded, called *Making Talismans, Amulets, and Charms for Protection and Profit*, that I had unearthed in a secondhand bookstore. The anonymous author had used badly drawn copies of the pentacles from the Key of Solomon and an alleged Atlantean language (which was suspiciously based on modern English letters) for his evocations.

With the enthusiasm of ignorance, I scratched the pentacle into a copper disk and then covered it with "barbarous names" of gods and angels of whom I had no concept. I then chanted a phrase four times over the mutilated metal in the indecipherable Atlantean language, which also meant nothing to me, and waited for the money to roll in.[1] After carrying the wretched disk around for a cashless six weeks, it finally dawned on me that that the talisman was not working.

It was not until I had been initiated into a mystery school some months later that the reason for this became clear. My teacher pointed out that talismans are more than pieces of metal with a few arcane drawings on them. They are living entities, batteries of magical power and force, and their creation is an ensoulment of energy.

At the time, I believed that such magic was beyond my skills and eagerly awaited adepthood where, plugged into the mysterious Akashic records, I would have access to all magical information and the Merlin-like ability to perform such great mystical feats. But the teaching about talismans in the various mystery schools in which I had been a member was sketchy, with little practical or specific information on their manufacture. It also took me a while to realize that my concept of adepthood was somewhat implausible.

Like many things in the esoteric world, it took a number of years for the ingredients for a coherent picture of how to manufacture talismans to emerge. This information came together suddenly from many different sources, and the resulting technique was in my hands.

A lot of this material owes much to a magical institution called the Esoteric Order of the Golden Dawn, which, in 1888, developed the most complex system of talisman manufacture.[2] Its adepts pooled together many of the ancient texts and techniques into a powerful, elaborate system. The Golden Dawn considered talisman making so important that progression within the Order was barred to a magician who could not make one work.

My reason for writing this book is to enable people to use talisman-making techniques safely and to return this art to the mainstream of modern occultism. It is possible for those with limited magical knowledge and experience to create effective talismans, amulets, and charms.

It is my belief that if these techniques are made public, people will have the ancient power of talismans in their own hands and can take responsibility for their own lives. This book examines various techniques of talisman making and provides the reader with the rituals necessary to consecrate them as living entities of power. With this knowledge comes the responsibility of using it wisely, of taking control of your own life and caring for your fellow human beings.

In this book, I cover a wide range of magical techniques. I approach them in a layered way, with each magical technique building on the last, until finally you, the reader, can design and empower the most simple or complex talisman.

By performing the practical exercises in each chapter, you will become increasingly attuned to the many divine and angelic beings that will turn the talisman from a simple piece of paper into a living being that works toward a particular magical goal. I include a few examples of different talismans, but, like many writers on occult subjects, I caution against attempting to manufacture them before performing the exercises in the earlier chapters. Talisman manufacture is not a superstitious shortcut to power and glory; it is a spiritual path in its own right. Making a talisman without understanding the principles of or having practical experience with the energies involved is like attempting brain surgery with a medical handbook in one hand and a scalpel in the other.

There are those who fear that people will use the information available in this book to harm others; but the magical beings named in this book, whose task it is to empower each talisman, are strong forces for the evolution of humanity, and it is impossible to coerce them into petty power plays. If these beings are not approached, or if they find a talisman's goal alien to their natures, then they will not allow it to work, and no harm will come to anyone.

The mere act of attempting to injure another magically will set in play strong karmic repercussions for the person who tries it. Ironically, the would-be black magicians or dark witches would be calling up the very beings who would be their judge and jury in the afterlife. For this reason, most sensible black magicians would not consider calling up beings of light to achieve the work of the night.[3]

Those of you who use the techniques in this book to help yourselves and others achieve true happiness will find you have the universe behind you.

---

1. I could have been saying "I call upon the powers of Jupiter" or "Do you have the pen of my aunt?" I suspect either would have gotten the same level of attention from the spirits.

2. Many people confuse the Esoteric Order of the Golden Dawn, which was founded in Britain in 1888, with the Hermetic Order of the Golden Dawn. The Esoteric Order folded at the turn of the twentieth century; the Hermetic Order was a name Israel Regardie invented when he revived it.

3. I am aware that the term "sensible black magician" is a contradiction in terms.

1

Talismans and How They Work

A talisman, amulet, or charm is *any physical object that stores and radiates a magical energy to create change.* A metallic disk, stone, wand, sword, pen, paper, or television remote control can be a talisman provided that it is dedicated toward a "magical purpose."[1] The definition of magic, however, has successfully eluded occultists for centuries.

Aleister Crowley, a Golden Dawn adept, devised the most widely accepted definition of magic. He argued that magic is "the science and art of causing change to occur in conformity with will," but this is too wide a definition to be of much use.[2] Crowley, himself, admitted that this definition implies that any willed act is magical. While turning on a light switch may be perceived as magical to someone who has not seen electricity, most would not define it as a magical act.

Another definition of magic, touted by more than one magical school of which I have been a member, is "the art of causing meaningful coincidences at will." This is equally unsatisfactory, though, since magical work does not always create coincidences that can be seen on the material plane.

While it is not entirely satisfactory either, my definition of magic is "the art and science of becoming a co-creator with a Supreme God."

This is not to say that we can be co-equal with the Most High, but rather that we merge into Divinity and its purpose. Occultism teaches that everyone has unlimited potential. We stop becoming successful only when we forget that we are part of an infinite creator. This divine creator aspect of us is like a divine secret self; Jung called it the Higher Self. As this self is realized, we become more in tune with the Divine and have access to more of its powers.[3]

Occult techniques bring us to a gradual realization of our immortal nature over a period of incarnations. In the early stages of occult training, we develop enough belief in its concepts to effect changes in our material surroundings.

Using my definition, a talisman, amulet, or charm is a material object that stores and transmits a fusion of the magician's will and universal powers to create something new.

How Talismans Work

To know how talismans, amulets, and charms work, it is important to know how things in the universe are created.

Like a physicist, an occultist defines the universe as being made up of energy vibrating at different frequencies. Occultists, however, say this energy is intelligent and is the material part of a single divine being. They go further to say that this energy extends to higher frequencies than have been identified by physicists.

Occultists define four frequencies or levels that exist within different dimensions of the same space (figure 1). These are sometimes called the four worlds of the Cabbalah. These worlds interact and affect each other. An event that happens on one level of creation will affect all the others. A form of Jewish mysticism called Cabbalah named these levels *Atziluth*, the world of deity; *Briah*, the world of creation; *Yetzirah*, the world of formation; and *Assiah*, the world of matter.

The highest frequency is the creative intelligence of the universe or a Supreme God. This is where all ideas in the universe are born.

These divine ideas filter down to the next level where they become an impulse toward a particular direction. At this level, the ancients noted that parts of God divided into specializations. For example, one specialization would be a creator and another a destroyer. The ancients named these divine specializations *archangels*.[4] If God's idea were to create dogs, then the archangel would map out the details of what would make up a dog and its evolutionary destiny.

Highest Frequency

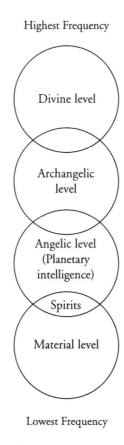

Lowest Frequency

Figure 1. The four worlds or levels of creation and how they interact.

The work of the archangels filters down to the next level. Here the divine plan is drawn in greater detail. The ancients noted that different parts of the archangel would specialize again into what they called *angels*. There was one angel for each part of the creation. Using the last example, there would be an angel responsible for creating each dog's teeth, another for its hair, and another for working out each animal's time of death.

Once this work has been carried out, the image of the dog is strong enough to manifest on the material plane. Here the images are formed, under the angel's instructions, out of beings called *elementals*. These creatures are partly built of spirit, but resonate to different types of matter and effectively build the image on the material level.

There are four types of elementals, which are described in terms of the type of matter they resemble. The lowest level of elementals are the earth elementals, or gnomes, which represent solids. Higher up are the water elementals, or undines, which represent liquids. The next highest are the air elementals, or sylphs, which represent gases. The highest level of elementals are the fire elementals, or salamanders, which represent radiant energy.

A talisman is like the foot of a ladder through the four worlds. It contacts the divine idea and the correct archangel, angel, and elemental builders. It continuously pours power into all four levels until the desired result takes place.

Making its physical design resonate to the forces that it is trying to contact makes the loading of the talisman easier. The talisman should be a color and shape that corresponds to the force that you wish to attract. It should have occult signs and divine names of power that occultists agree are the earthly representations of the four worlds, and it should be made at a time when those powers are the strongest.

We will be looking at talisman designs in chapter 3. The technique we will use will utilize the colors, angels, and names of power used in a Cabbalistic glyph called the Tree of Life. This glyph, which is the basis of Jewish esoteric tradition, has influenced countless Jewish and Christian talisman makers for centuries, especially those in magical orders like the Esoteric Order of the Golden Dawn.

Claiming Your Power to Build a Talisman

It is possible to build powerful magical objects because we exist simultaneously on all four levels and can become consciously aware of each of them. Like a deity, we can formulate a creation and then work with the archangels, angels, and elementals to build it on Earth. With this power, we theoretically create whatever situation we want. We do this instinctively every day.

If we have this power, then why do we experience so much suffering? Surely we would create environments that are happy and prosperous.

The problem is that the creative process is forged by the unconscious beliefs of each of us. Most of us unconsciously believe that our lives will remain the same or get worse. We worry about bad things happening to us, and our moments of happiness are spoiled with the fear that everything will be taken away.

Psychological fears and phobias built by environmental conditioning add more bogus beliefs to the mix so that most of us use our magical powers to build a hell on Earth rather than creating a happy environment.

Occultists are in the process of reclaiming the use of their creative powers. Unfortunately, this is easier said than done. The psychological blocks to our success are not always embedded in one lifetime, but in many incarnations. Even after all our personal blocks are resolved, there are the complexes shared by all humans—however spiritually developed we may be.

It is hard to be successful in magic without first removing our psychic blocks; however, success in magic often removes these blocks. Nothing succeeds like success. Magicians who have used talismans to improve their environment are more likely to believe that such techniques will improve their future.

What is the way out of the catch-22? The ancients used ritual magic to bypass that which stands in the way of success.

How Ritual Works

Ceremonial magic is a drama in which a magician plays the main character. His stage is set in a candle-lit room, with thick, sweet-smelling incense, and usually an altar; but the magician's mind is far away.

The magician is imagining that his ritual is taking place in a mystical temple in sun-scorched Egypt or on top of a sacred mountain. In his mind's eye, he calls to beings that exist in other worlds and imagines that they arrive.

As the magician loses himself in the drama of the ritual, something strange happens. The illusion becomes real. The magician feels like the gods and angels that he called feel are really there. Energy can be seen crisscrossing the room, which is charged with a strange atmosphere.

The ritual magician can enter an altered state of consciousness. He becomes aware of the next world, and, in his mind, operates upon it. He has effectively laid a new reality over this one. It is a reality where he talks to gods and goddesses because he is like a god or goddess. Because this altered reality flows down the worlds, an observer with no psychic ability often sees things that are not on the material level.

Because these worlds are built of thought, the language the magician uses are symbols and images. The ritual act of drawing a pentagram in the air has a reality in realms of thought. Symbolic systems have the power to take the magician to even higher states of consciousness.

There is a further advantage. Once the magician is walking in the realms of the angels, he can cooperate with them to change patterns of creation. It is easier to make changes in the worlds above this one. They are made out of thought and can be controlled by thought. Immediately after they have been placed in the worlds above, the changes flow downward until they have a material reality.

These are the acts of a high-level magician, but even a novice can obtain staggering effects from the most basic ritual without hitting deep altered states.

This happens for two reasons. The first reason is because of the great occult maxim "As above, so below, and as below, so above." This statement (which was written in an early Hermetic treatise called the "Emerald Tablet") implies that everything that happens on Earth also happens on the other frequencies or levels of creation and vice versa; so a simple ritual actually does stir the angelic levels.

Simple rituals also work because they can unlock potential from us that is so subliminal that we never knew we had it.

One talisman consecration ritual only requires a colored candle to be plunged into a bowl of water as a simple ritual phrase is spoken. Having tested a talisman consecrated by this ritual, I discovered that it is as effective a talisman as those made by more elaborate means.

The reason that this ritual works so well is that it focuses the magician's concentration on the task at hand. This focus sets up a vortex on all planes of manifestation, drawing astral beings toward the magician's goal.

Some of the simpler talisman systems work because the angelic contacts, whose job it is to empower it, have agreed to let it work that way. Countless magicians and Wiccans have used this ritual and each success has added to its power. When you use this ritual, it is like you have been given a key that bypasses the need for a large amount of technical knowledge.

This ritual's weak point, however, is its simplicity. Many people find that they cannot work with such rituals because they don't believe anything that simple will work. This attitude prevents the ritual from achieving its goal.

That which is built from thought can be destroyed by another contradictory thought. It is useless to spend hours performing a ritual to earn yourself money if at the end of it you say things like "This will never work, nothing good ever happens to me." You have to suspend disbelief and believe you will get the result you want until long after the ritual has ended. Only after you have gotten your result, or realized that the ritual has not worked, should you analyze it too closely.

This is one of the reasons why occult orders insist on secrecy and keep silent about their ritual activities. If you tell someone that you have performed a ritual, then you are dependent on them not to have negative thoughts about its success and accidentally destroy your results. Since this cannot be guaranteed, it is always better to keep quiet about it.

Later in this book, we will examine different types of talisman consecration rituals.

Reasons to Build Talismans

Theoretically, it is possible to make a talisman for any magical purpose—certainly those that have survived the passage of time do not give any indication that their tasks were limited. Talismans have been created for esoteric reasons like spiritual development, to help the soul transverse the afterlife, and more mundane tasks like helping someone sing properly.

Many of these tasks could be performed equally well by an act of ritual magic; however, there are some advantages for creating a talisman, even for an established ritual magician.

A ritual targets those three levels above the material with a single mental image and aims for an eventual physical result as the wish percolates downward. A ritual is generally a one-shot technique that either works or fails. A talisman, however, draws magical power all the way down the levels and connects it to the earth plane extremely effectively. A talisman keeps the doors to these levels open over a long period of time and organically draws the right circumstances to it, while repelling negative suggestions. To achieve the same effect, a magician would have to do many rituals regularly.[5]

Another advantage of making a talisman is that while a ritual is usually performed in a secret place, a talisman can be carried to the scene where it is most needed. If a traveler wants protection, by carrying the talisman with him, it can work directly with the minds of those who might attack him.

One magician, who was having trouble with his boss, made a talisman so that his boss would leave him alone. He taped the talisman underneath the lid of his boss' desk. Every working day, his boss was exposed to the energy radiating from the talisman, and he did leave the magician alone.

Talismans have also been made for writers to help the creative energies flow into their work. A friend of mine who is a writer has a talisman beside his computer that he touches whenever he experiences "writer's block."

The tactile nature of talismans is one of the key reasons that they are so popular. You can make talismans for friends, who are then constantly reminded of the work you have done for him or her. When they touch the talisman, they unconsciously cooperate with the energies that it represents. People who are sick will feel reassured knowing that a healing talisman is under their pillow, slowing enabling the changes in their bodies to make them well again.

On a more cynical level, a talisman provides some material proof that a ritual has been performed. Historically, a layperson would not want to hand over large amounts of cash to a magician or priest to perform a ritual unless some material result was seen.

A less technological culture would allow people to see their shaman go into a trance and dance about while possessed by the spirits; however, secrecy of magicians and witches prevents people from entering their circles or lodges to see the work that they have commissioned being carried out. For some reason, people who walk away with a charm or a piece of paper with Cabbalistic signs written on it feel that they have gotten something for their money.

The purpose of a talisman is often something general, like healing, wealth, influence, or protection. This has led some to say that a talisman should be for a general purpose, while a ritual is for something specific, but this is not always the case; at times, the aim of a talisman is specifically identified.

I tend to make talismans for the following reasons:

- When power needs to be brought to bear on the situation over time and there are a large number of factors that will need to be brought into line before the desired physical result manifests.

- When nonmagical people ask for my help and may not believe that anything will happen unless they have something tangible to hold.[6]

- When exposure to the talisman's energies is a key component in getting the desired result. For example, the energy of a healing talisman often works on the patient at a cellular level and thus needs to be in close proximity to him or her.

- When placement of power in a different location will help bring about the desired result. One occult order in New Zealand buried a talisman in the ground next to the road just before an intersection that was a local accident black spot. Every time a driver approached the intersection, the talisman would cause him or her to take extra care. Following the order's action, there was some reduction in accidents at that intersection, although the talisman had no effect on drunken drivers.

Planetary Influences

We will be looking at several different types of talismans in this book, but we will mostly use the energies of the seven main "planets" of the ancients—the Sun, the Moon, Mercury, Venus, Mars, Jupiter, and Saturn. It seems odd that, in a developing science like occultism, we seem reluctant to embrace energies of the recently discovered planets Uranus, Neptune, and Pluto. The truth is, though, that the energies from these seven bodies can be used to get everything talisman makers could want.

Dion Fortune, a magician and writer who set up her own magic order in the late 1920s, once described the planets as the physical bodies of beings of extremely complex energies. These planetary beings orbit the aura of the Sun, which is the higher self of the solar system. Together they make a huge physical body of a living being that we call the solar system. Like the energy centers described in the magical systems of India and China, the planets are vortexes of energy for this solar system's body.

Each center has a special function; for example, Venus provides the love force and the energies of creativity.

These vortexes bombard the other centers with their unique energies, creating and effecting change upon them. Fortune said that it is these fields of energy that have enabled Earth to develop and evolve life. It was this rare condition that enabled the Divine to send a life wave of divine sparks to incarnate and evolve among this matter, and it was these divine sparks that became human.[7]

Whether or not you accept this rationalization, it shows how important the planets are considered to be by the working occultist. A planetary talisman aims to form a vortex to capture more of the planetary energy than is normal. It then takes this energy and directs it toward your heart's desire.

A magician wishing to make a talisman would decide which planetary energy would match the talisman's purpose and would then build one that would attract that particular force.

Each planet is listed below with its attributions. To figure out which planet you should use, think about what you specifically want your talisman to do. If you want to find the right sort of house, you would use a Saturn talisman. If you want protection from a bully, you would use a Mars talisman.

Saturn

Fate, time, the past, limits and boundaries, form, structures including houses, old age, serious, ambition, bones, knees, skeleton, shins, ankles and circulation, rheumatism, arthritis, envy, suffering, fear, guilt, toxins, repressed aspects of the self, death, vermin and lice, politicians, scientists, architects, teachers, mines, mountains, and wastelands.

Jupiter

Lawmaking, opportunity, growth, progress, evolution, money, banks, rulers, royalty, faith, hope, charity, redemption, freedom, spiritual wisdom and development, hypocrisy, hips, thighs, feet, lawyers, priests, counselors, actors, open spaces, public places, and panoramic views.

Mars

Wars, anger, action, sexual desire, physical energy, quarrels, courts, justice, courage, protection, transformation, revenge, destruction, surgery, the head, genitals, excretory system, rashes, red spots, migraine, predators, soldiers, surgeons, athletes, furnaces, foundries, and metal work.

Venus

Love, eroticism, desire, pleasure, inspiration, joy, partnerships, peace, laughter, friendship, creativity, the arts, beauty, evaluation, promiscuity, overindulgence, lewdness, gentle animals, the throat and neck, kidneys, lower back, diplomacy, artists, fashions, bedrooms, and gardens.

Mercury

Communication, movement, messages, computers, the media, language, trade, theft, magic, skill, learning, intellect, psychology as a science, science, rationality, cunning and mischievous animals like monkeys, the digestive system, arms and hands, merchants, clerks, accountants, scholars, universities, examinations, shops, schools, airports, and train and bus stations.

Moon

The unconscious, habits, instinct, sea, rhythm, the astral realm, mysteries, women (particularly their health), mothers, childbirth, psychism, menstruation, mental health, the stomach, breasts, warts, sterility, obsessions, delusions, insanity, cleaners, brewers, midwives, sailors, and harbors.

The Sun

Leadership, general health, healing, organization, arrogance, display, drama, fathers, power, individualization, the heart, the back, the lungs, kings, directors, managers, actors, palaces, and theaters.

Most magicians make healing talismans using the Sun, as this aligns well with Raphael the angelic healer; however, each planet rules a certain part of the body, and many complaints are caused by pathology of that particular planetary energy. A talisman of an appropriate planet provides a correct template of the energy with which the body can heal itself—it also uses the healing function of other lesser known angels.

1. A *talisman* is the generic term. An *amulet* is a talisman that is specifically designed to protect the wearer. A *charm* is the "spell" that empowers the talisman; however, over the years it has also come to denote a talismanic object that is usually worn on a necklace or bracelet.

2. Aleister Crowley's book *Magic in Theory and Practice* dedicates thirteen pages of the Introduction to his definition of magic. See Aleister Crowley, *Magic in Theory and Practice* (New York, NY: Dover Publications, 1976) xii–xxiii.

3. Much of this process takes place after the incarnation process. There are great adepts, or Bodhisattvas (in the Buddhist tradition), who are carrying on their evolution, progressively becoming more godlike, after incarnation.

4. Although I am using the terms of the Jewish and Christian hierarchies, many religions carry a fourfold hierarchical structure. In ancient Egypt, there was the creator god Atum; major gods like Isis, Osirus, and Horus; and lesser gods like the domestic god Bes.

5. There are some rituals that are repeated over a long period of time to achieve this effect. However, they tend to be significant workings that work on a large scale, like the development of humanity, rather than the more personal functions that talismans perform.

6. It is a magical rule that you don't intervene in someone else's life unless he or she asks you to do so.

7. See Dion Fortune, *Cosmic Doctrine* (Wellingborough: Aquarian, 1988) chapters 6–9.

2

A Brief History of Talismans

In the beginning, ancient people believed in the living powers of talismans. Whether it was the bone of an ancient ancestor used to hold back the evil spirits in a storm, or the crudely carved, large-breasted goddess statue that was appeased to promote fertility, a talisman was an earthly object that had somehow become a god, a power, a spirit, or the focus of divine energy.

Anthropologists looking for the roots of religions have found startling similarities between early magical beliefs of cultures around the world. The people of these cultures had a strong belief in life after death and believed that ancestors could be contacted to assist the living. Some tribal cultures insisted that their ancestors had a direct influence on their daily existence and could bring good or bad fortune according to their mood.

There was vibrancy in what these ancient people believed. Their surroundings were alive. The trees, the sea, rivers, and the animals all had spirits. If the ancients had abstract gods, they were usually personifications of these spirits—they were storm gods, gods of the wind and rain, the sleeping mountain, the corn, the harvest, or the stars.

Standing between the tribe, these powerful spirits, and the ancestors was the shaman.[1] He was a walker between the levels of creation who could travel to the spirit world and talk to all these forces for the good of the tribe. Ronald Hutton, a professor of history at Bristol University and an expert on the shaman of Siberia, explained to me in an interview that the would-be shaman was selected by the spirits to be their spokesperson. Because of the stress involved, it was not a task for a volunteer, and candidates usually had to be driven kicking and screaming by the spirits and tribe into their new vocation.

The main talismanic tools of a Siberian shaman were a drum and robe. Both were made from the hide of an animal that was spiritually linked to the shaman.

"The shaman would go out into the wild and find an animal that they felt most attracted to and make the drum skin and robe from its hide," said Professor Hutton. "Likewise, the wood of the drum, which was supposed to come from the world tree, would be selected from the forest because it looked a little different from all the rest."[2]

The shamans would consecrate the items by singing magical songs. These charms were either passed down from shaman to pupil, or given as a gift from the spirits. The drum would be painted with images of the different levels of the world, and the robe would be decorated with magical metal statues.

Professor Hutton said that these talismanic tools were vital for the shaman's journeys to the spirit world: "The drum was the shaman's horse. Its beat was the steed's footfalls, which carried them in flight to the other world. The robe covered, protected, and empowered the shaman for the flight."

So powerful were these talismanic objects that, if it was not possible to give them to another shaman on the death of the owner, they were treated like toxic chemicals. The magical equipment was either buried or hung in a tree with the owner's body in sacred ground that no one went near.[3]

"The belief was that they remained charged with power forever. If the drum and robe were touched by someone who was unprepared, the spirits would destroy them out of self-defense," said Professor Hutton.

Ancient Egypt

The next phase of development of Western talismans came from ancient Egypt. Here, the talismans and amulets were developed into a format that many would recognize.

In Egypt, the magicians or priests aspired to assume the form of a god or goddess in their magic. Long evocations described the powers of the god, which threw the magicians into such reverie that they believed they had these powers. When they felt this divine power flow through them, they would concentrate it into the talismans.

The magicians were helped by the magical use of writing. Hieroglyphic words and pictures of the gods' names controlled the gods and concentrated their power to the point that the very letters radiated energy.

Each god and goddess had myths associated with him or her. These myths contained elements that were common to ordinary people. For example, Isis controlled snakes in order to discover the Sun god Ra's secret name; her husband, Osirus, overcame death and was reborn; Horus the hawk-faced god defeated crocodiles and hippopotami; and Thoth the ibis-headed god invented writing.

The Egyptians believed that if they identified with a god, they would receive a cure or protection similar to the god's (or goddess') mythic ability. The story of Isis, Osirus, and Horus was one of the key tales that spawned the manufacture of talismans for ancient Egyptians.

In this myth, the god Osirus and his sister, Isis, ruled Egypt successfully; but Osirus' brother, Set, murdered him and hacked his body into pieces. Isis gathered the body together, except for the penis, which was eaten by a fish.

Making him a golden penis, Isis resurrected Osirus long enough for her to conceive a son and heir. Horus the avenger was born and eventually slew Set.

The Egyptians believed that if they knew a creature's "true" name, they had power over it. Isis was a powerful magician who knew the name of all creatures. She used this power to protect Horus until he could meet and kill Set.

In their book *Egypt*, Vivian Davies and Renee Friedman observed that, around 700 B.C., small stone tablets showing Horus holding snakes and scorpions and standing on crocodiles were very popular. It was believed that if you poured water on the "charged" stone, the stone would empower the water to make a tonic to cure snake and scorpion bites.

Another Egyptian way of avoiding attacks was to worship and appease the gods who might strike them, like the snake god Meretseger and the scorpion goddess

Selket. The Egyptians built clay snakes as talismans of protection not only against reptiles but also against the nightmares caused by demonic forces.

One of the most famous protection talismans was the eye of Horus. Horus lost his eye in a battle with Set, but Thoth the wisdom god was able to replace it. This "eye," when worn, was able to protect the wearer from the attacks of Set and demons that caused sickness. According to Davies and Friedman, it symbolized the Egyptian belief that righteous living and wisdom would defeat any illness.

Amulets to protect children were common, particularly in later periods. These were long, cylindrical objects (usually made of metal) contained a narrow roll of papyrus with a text in which three deities promise to protect the child. This one, which is in the British Museum, was written for a girl:

> *We shall keep her safe from Sakhmet and her son. We shall keep her safe from the collapse of a wall or the fall of a thunderbolt.*
> *We shall keep her safe from leprosy, from blindness through-out her whole life-time.*[4]

Talismans were an important part of the rituals for the mummification of the dead. Models of scarabs, which were Egyptian beetles closely linked to the Sun and resurrection, were placed in the mummy wrappings to protect the dead. The most important was the scarab talisman, which was placed over the heart. The Egyptian magical manual *The Book of Coming Forth by Day*, commonly called *The Book of the Dead*, described how the heart scarab was consecrated.

A man who was clean and pure, who had not eaten meat or fish or had sex, should make the heart scarab from green stone with a rim plated with gold. He should then say the following:

> *My heart of my mother. My heart of my mother. My heart-case of my transforma-tions. Let not any one stand up to bear testimony against me . . . Let no one make thee to fall away from me in the presence of the Keeper of the Balance. Thou art my Ka, the dweller in my body, the god Khnemu who makest sound my members. Mayest thou appear in the place of happiness whither we go. Let not make my name to stink Shenit Chiefs, who make men to be stable. Let it be satisfactory unto*

us, and let the listening be satisfactory unto us, and let there be joy of heart to us at the weighing of words. Let not lies be told against me before the Great God, the Lord of Amentet. Verily, how great shalt thou be when thou risest up in triumph![5]

This talisman prevented the heart from testifying against the dead person during the final judgment of the soul.

Other scarabs had magical spells or symbols engraved on the back of them. Sometimes these engravings were the names of the owner linking them to the regenerative powers of the insect, and other times they were phrases like "Amon is my strength" or "Strong is the heart."

Mummies wore necklaces with the eye of Horus, and their tombs contained small statues of deities designed to protect them from demons. The heads of the four sons of Horus protected Canopic jars, which contained the dead person's stomach, intestines, lungs, and liver.

Another important talismanic object, which was placed under the mummy's head, was a talisman made of linen stiffened with plaster and inscribed with pictures of the gods. Called a *hypocephalus*, it kept the body warm in the afterlife. The Egyptians had a prayer to Amon that was probably recited when the talisman was consecrated:

I am the Hidden One in the hidden place. I am a perfect spirit among the companions of Ra and I have come forth among perfect souls … I am one of the spirits that have come forth from the underworld: grant unto me the things my body needs and heaven for my soul and a hidden place for my mummy.

The ankh was another popular amulet. It was a prime symbol for eternity and was carried by many gods in temple wall paintings.

Greek and Roman Influences

Alexander the Great's annexation of Egypt in November 332 B.C. led to dramatic changes in the development of talismans. The founding of the great library in Alexandra by Alexander's successor, Ptolemy Soter, in approximately 283 B.C., created a mecca for philosophers, magicians, priests, and scientists. Many of the texts and maps of the known world were copied and stored at this library.

The city was extremely cosmopolitan, and from this culture of knowledge was born the Hermetic and Gnostic movements. These were people who believed it was important to "know God," and they forged many complex and esoteric ways of doing so. These movements influenced the Christian and Jewish faiths; in fact, many scholars believe that someone influenced by Gnostic terminology wrote John's gospel during the first century.

Upon the death of the last pharoah of Egypt, Cleopatra, in 30 B.C., Egypt became another Roman province. By this stage, the Egyptians had largely forgotten the meaning of their more detailed hieroglyphics. Many spoke Greek and wrote in a mixture of Greek and Egyptian scripts called Coptic.

Talismans were generally written on papyrus or engraved on metal, usually lead. The magical words engraved upon them were a mixture of bastardized Egyptian and Greek. There was heavy use of "barbarous names of power," which are indecipherable names with lots of vowels. The seven Greek vowels were believed to possess special powers. The Egyptian language was made up entirely of consonants, so the Egyptians were intrigued by the ability of vowels to animate words. These long names, which were often made entirely of vowels, were chanted or sung during the Gnostic magic rites and religious rituals.

A healing talisman from the third century A.D. has this inscription:

rbath agrammê fiblô chnêmeô

a e êêê iiii ooooo uuuuuu ôôôôôô

Lord Gods heal Helena daughter of. . . .

From every illness

and every shivering and fever.

ephemeral, quotidan, tertian, quartan

iarbath, agrammê fiblô chnêmeô

aeêiouôôuoiêea

eêiouôôuoiêe

êiouôôuoiê

ouôôuo

uôôu uuuuu

ôô

Talismans in the British Museum representing this time in history include the drawings of strange multiple gods of the Gnostics. For example, Abraxas has the head of a rooster, the body of a man, and the legs of a snake.

The British Museum also contains popular talismans with the gods depicted as foot soldiers or riders trampling demons. These images, which were often carried by Roman soldiers, were supposed to ward off evil.

Another technique to deflect evil was to write the words of a talisman in a triangle of decreasing or increasing letters. This made something either go away or draw close. By using the same technique in modern English, a boil could be made to disappear by writing this:

Boil

Boi

Bo

B

An ancient magician who wanted God to draw close would write this:

A

EE

HHH

I I I I

OOOOO

ΥΥΥΥΥ

ωωωωωωω

The Greeks developed a system of talismanic cursing. A curse containing the name of the victim was written on a lead tablet known as a *Katadesmoi*, which means "binding formula."[6] This was thrown into graves, pits, or wells, thus handing the victim over to demons and the ghosts of the dead. These cursing and binding tablets seem to be an invention unique to the Greeks. Used in Greece beginning in the fifth century B.C., their use soon spread throughout the Greek and Roman lands.

The preparation of katadesmoi later entailed rituals similar to the popular conception of voodoo magic. This included the binding or burning of wax, clay, or lead "voodoo" dolls, which represented the victim.

One love spell preserved in the University of Michigan's papyrus collection was written in the second century by someone named Ailourion who wanted a woman named Kopria to desire and love him:

I deposit this binding spell with you, chthonian gods—Pluto and Kore. . . . Bind Kopria, whom her mother Taesis bore, the hair of whose head you have, for Ailourion, whom his mother named Kopria bore, that she may not submit to vaginal nor anal intercourse, nor gratify another youth or another man except Ailourion only, whom his mother named Kopria bore, and that she may not even be able to eat nor drink nor ever get sleep nor enjoy good health nor have peace in her soul or mind in her desire for Ailourion, whom his mother Kopria bore, until Kopria, whom her mother Taesis bore, whose hair you have, will spring up from every place and every house, burning with passion, and come to Ailourion, whom his mother named Kopria bore, loving and adoring with all her soul, with all her spirit, with unceasing and unremitting and constant erotic binding, Ailourion, whom his mother named Kopria bore, with a divine love, from this very day, from the present hour, for the rest of Kopria's life.[7]

The use of katadesmoi did not always have such a dark purpose. Lead disks asking the gods for healing were often deposited in the sacred wells or lakes. A large number of these types of katadesmoi have been uncovered in the English town of Bath, which had a temple dedicated to Minerva, who guarded its sacred springs.

As Christianity took hold of the Roman Empire in the second and third century, its Gnostic variations were dubbed a heresy and therefore suppressed. There seems to be no evidence, though, that interest in talismans slackened. Many examples of talismans exist today with images and invocations to Christ and the angels.

One of these, in the Kelsey Museum, shows a man spearing a lioness with a human female face. An angel blesses the rider with his raised wing. It is inscribed with the words "One God who conquers evil; He who dwells in the help of the Most High will abide in the shelter of the God of heaven." On the reverse side is Christ enthroned and surrounded by the four animals of the Apocalypse—an ox, a man, an eagle, and a lion. It is inscribed with the words "Holy, Holy, Holy, Lord Sabaôth" and "The seal of the living God, Guard from every evil him who carries this amulet."[8]

Christianity developed its own talismanic items, particularly around the cult of the saints. Bones and other artifacts associated with the saints were often associated with miracles. During the Middle Ages, a church with an appropriate relic would be a site for pilgrimages from the faithful who hoped that the saint would grant them a miracle—usually some form of healing.

Pilgrimages were a lucrative trade for churches who often fought over, and sometimes fabricated, holy relics. One story tells how a bishop visited a cathedral that was famous for owning the skeleton of Mary Magdalene. He joined the queue of pilgrims who were kissing the sacred skeleton. When it was his turn, he bit a chunk off the bone and carried it back to his church where it, too, attracted pilgrims.

One of the most famous religious talismans was the True Cross upon which Christ was supposed to have been crucified. Bits of this relic passed back and forth between the warring forces during the Crusades.

There were many enterprising Christians who sold sailcloth from St. Peter's boat, Jesus' swaddling clothes, and bones from any particular saint. Occultists, myself included, who examined some of these talismanic objects in the early 1990s, particularly those that had been adopted by the church, testify that the objects do develop a power of their own. Two occultists, Marian Green and John Mathews, acknowledged the power that emanates from such items in their book *The Grail Seeker's Companion*. When referring to a relic alleged to be Christ's blood, kept in the Church of the Holy Blood in Bruges, Belgium, Green and Mathews said:

> It looks like dry red dust inside its glass container—but it radiates energy. At least one of the authors can testify to the extraordinary power of the realisations made in meditation in the beautiful medieval church which is its home.[9]

My own theory is that the consecrating power of the belief of so many faithful has enabled a medieval con trick to become a powerful religious item.

It was among the Jews that talisman-making grew into a scientific art, and it is their work that has influenced the Western magical tradition the most.

Jewish Talismans

It is clear that we owe more to the Jewish tradition of talisman making than any other. It is fair to say that within Jewish communities the technique of making talismans has been consistent for several thousand years.

In his book *Hebrew Amulets*, T. Schrire says that Hebrew talismans were considered to be so effective during the Middle Ages that they were bought by Christians. Ironically, many Christian knights who persecuted Jews in their homeland looked to these same Jews to provide them with magical protection during the Crusades.

Orthodox Jews frowned on the use of talismans, mostly because they were opposed to anything that even hinted of magic. They were suspicious of the secrecy of many talisman makers and feared that there could be some form of idolatrous practice involved in talisman making.

Despite this, there was some pressure on Jewish leaders to produce talismans, and many found loopholes within the Jewish law to create them. By the time the Jews returned from their captivity in Babylon, talismans had become an accepted part of daily life. Jewish literature, or Mishnah, defined different "grades" of talismans. Those made by an expert could be carried on the Sabbath. Curiously, it was considered improper to use a talisman for healing, but it was acceptable to prevent illness with one. It is rare to find a Hebrew talisman with the word "cure" on it, but there are some talismans that ask that a person be "protected from" a variety of illnesses.[10]

Jewish talismans gained their power because they were made using Hebrew letters and phrases from the Bible, which contained what were considered the words of God. The main difference between Hebrew talismans and those of other cultures is the lack of images other than symbols and an almost total dependence on Hebrew letters and names to provide power.

In the Bible, there are many different names, or shemoth, given to "God." The most famous is יהוה, which Christian scholars transliterated to JHVH or Jehovah. It literally means "he is" or "he will be." The Jews considered this name too holy to pronounce and replaced it with others like Adonai, which the Christians translated as "Lord."

There are other names mentioned in the Bible, like El, Shaddai, Elohim, Yah, and so on. Others were added by taking the first letters of key Bible verses and making new ones. This technique was called Notarikon, and the classic example of this was the seventy-two-lettered name of God called Shem Hameforash.[11] This "name" was taken from Exodus 14:19–21. In the original Hebrew, each of these three verses consists of seventy-two letters. Shem Hameforash was made by making a composite of three verses by taking the first letters of the first verse, another letter from the second verse, and the first letter of the third verse to make the syllables of the name.

Each name represented a different aspect of God, and each Hebrew talisman began with a prayer to one of them like "In the name of Adonai" or "With the help of Shaddai." The purpose of this was to remind the owner that although he or she wanted protection against a certain act, it was through the power of God that it would come about—God still made the final decision.

Talismans also evoked angels, and there were thousands of these to choose from. We will be looking at their use in talisman making in chapter 4. The most common angels on Hebrew talismans were Uriel, Raphael, Gabriel, Michael, and Nuriel. The names of these angels were sometimes abbreviated to a single name of power using Notarikon. According to Schrire, the name ארגמנ, Argaman, was fairly common and was constructed by taking the first letter of the name of each angel.

After choosing the appropriate God and angel names, the talisman maker would select a Bible verse that was relevant to the talisman's purpose. By taking these verses, often shortened by Notarikon, it was believed that that God's power was being stamped onto the talisman.

In choosing a Bible verse to construct a talisman for a good singing voice, Exodus 15:1 was considered one of the best. This verse says, "Then sang Moses and the children of Israel this song unto the Lord, for he hath triumphed gloriously: the horse and his rider hath he thrown into the sea."

Sometimes the choice of Bible verse was esoteric or cryptic. For example, Genesis 49:22 appears on a large number of talismans designed to ward off evil; yet this verse is, "Joseph is a fruitful bough, even a fruitful bough by a well; whose branches run over a wall."

After the Bible verse, a short prayer was inscribed, depending on the amount of space. Then the talisman inscription ended with a direct statement of what it was supposed to do, i.e., "Let N, who bears this talisman upon him, sing with a sweet voice." It is common to see the word *Amen* repeated three times and then the word *selah* three times on many traditional Jewish talismans.

Jewish talismans were made of metal disks or written on paper. Some of the metal amulets had red beads attached as this color was considered protective. Judging by the amount of mistakes in lettering and names that metal workers made when constructing talismans, it is fair to believe that most did not know what they were doing. Skilled scribes wrote the few paper talismans that have survived. They constructed them with the same care and skill they lavished on copying the Bible.

One instruction demanded that the talisman be written while in prayer or fasting. As the maker dipped his pen in prepared ink, he was instructed to say, "In the name of Shaddai who created heaven and Earth I write this name for . . ." and then the purpose of the talisman. Once finished, he was to say, "Blessed are thou, O Lord, who has sanctified thy great name and revealed it to thy pious ones to show its power and might in the language in the writing of it and in the utterance of the mouth."[12]

It is not surprising that since talisman writing required so much piety, it was often left to the chief rabbi of a town to perform. The Jewish saint Rabbi Haim Joseph David Azulai (1724–1807) made his living by selling talismans, which he constructed using his extensive Cabbalistic knowledge. He wrote extensively on suitable angels, Bible verses, and codes for use in talismans, and after his death his signature was considered talismanic.

Mystical writings, particularly the Cabbalah, had a strong influence on the development of talismans. Here, the names of God and angels were codified for practical use.

In 1230, Eleazar of Worms wrote the most significant book on the manufacture of Jewish talismans. His book, *Sefer Raziel*, which was written in the Middle Ages, was not published until 1701. This did not stop its wide circulation among Jews in manuscript form. The book had an impact on the Jewish sect the Hassidics, who had been prolific talisman makers.

Sefer Raziel included different sorts of mystical alphabets that were designed to make the meaning of the text cryptic to all but the initiated. It also included detailed lists of angels, symbols, and Bible verses. These created talismans that were much more elaborate, but it was essentially the same formula that Jewish talisman makers had been using for centuries.

The amulet in figure 2 contains many different divine names. In the four corners, there are the four rivers of paradise. These were mentioned in the Book of Genesis as the Pison, Gihon, Hiddekel, and Euphrates, and were taken by the Cabbalists to represent the flowing of divine energy into creation.

On the circumference of the circle are the names associated with childbirth: Adam and Eve, Hutz, Lilith, Shamriel, Hasdiel, Sinvai, Sansanvai, and Semanglof. There is a

Figure 2. Sefer Raziel amulet for childbirth.

fourteen-letter name of God, a cut-down version of Psalm 91:11, and the words Amen and Selah.[13] On the outside of the hexagram is a forty-two-lettered name of God, and within the hexagon is Exodus 11:8.[14]

The first talisman made using a printing press was published in Venice in the sixteenth century. Printed talismans have remained more or less the same ever since. The writing inscribed was, "In the name of Shaddai," and asks for the protection of the bearer, who was never named. Bible verses were usually derived from Psalm 121 or

91. Although some printed talismans were consecrated or blessed by a rabbi, most were superstitiously believed to hold power by virtue of the Hebrew writing. Talisman making was a religious and creative act between the maker and the Almighty, but there is divine power in Hebrew writing, and the belief of the talisman's owner in the power of the letters can give a consecration of sorts.

Hebrew talismanic production, whether printed or handmade, is still fairly common. Most of them are written on pieces of parchment two by twenty inches in size and are tightly rolled and kept in containers. A friend of mine gave me one to protect me when I travel. It has a red cord and is kept rolled up in a transparent, straw-shaped plastic case.

One Jewish talismanic system that deserves a mention is the *Book of the Sacred Magic of Abramelin the Mage*. This book, which was written in the fifteenth century, describes a complete system of magic where the magician spends six months in retreat carrying out ritual practices before encountering his higher self and gaining mastery of his demons. These demons, and angels, empower a series of magical squares. Although magic squares were used in Jewish and Christian magical talismans, the Abramelin squares were unlike anything that had yet been produced. Figure 3 is an example of one that was used to find ancient medals and coins.

O	R	I	O	N
R	A	V	R	O
I	V	A	V	I
O	R	V	A	R
N	O	I	R	O

Figure 3. An Abramelin talisman to find medals and coins.

The Abramelin magical system had little influence on talisman development until the head of the Esoteric Order of the Golden Dawn, S. L. MacGregor Mathers, translated the only copy of the manuscript from medieval French. Some members of the Golden Dawn, particularly those in New Zealand, considered the squares to be extremely powerful. Aleister Crowley considered the squares to be so dangerous that he recommended keeping the book in a lead box. Many talisman makers believed that it was not sensible to use the squares unless you adopted the whole Abramelin magical system—which included the six-month retreat and achieving knowledge and conversation with your holy guardian angel.

Jewish influences crept into the Western magical tradition during the European Renaissance, and it is there that we have to look to find the next evolution in talisman making.

Talisman Making During the European Renaissance

After a thousand years of church-dominated learning, the dawn of the European Renaissance marked a revival in interest in the ancients and their teachings. Not only did the invention of the printing press in the middle of the fifteenth century lead to humanist reforms in education and science, it also helped disseminate esoteric and occult teachings.

In Italy, the ruler of Florence, Lorenzo de Medici (1478–1521), gave protection and employment to occultists like Giovanni Pico della Mirandola (1463–1494) and Marsilio Ficino (1433–1499). Mirandola and Ficino spent much of their lives researching Hebrew, Latin, and Greek manuscripts to bring new Neo-Platonic and Hermetic learning upon the world.

Mirandola was fascinated by the Cabbalah, which he regarded as a fulfillment of Christian religion. He did much to publicize the basics of this system among Christians, which also kindled their interest in Jewish talisman making.

The Greater Key of Solomon

One of the most important influences on magic at this time was a text called *The Greater Key of Solomon*, somtimes just called *The Key of Solomon*. This magical text was passed to Renaissance magicians in various formats from the Middle Ages. It was unlikely to have been published, as the Church would have most certainly banned it. Alongside the usual spell recipes and ritual practices, *The Key of Solomon* gives pages of planetary "pentacles" for use in different spells (figure 4).

Hebrew is used on the talismans. They bear similarities to traditional Jewish talismans, including divine names, Bible verses, magic squares, and angels; however, they also include Gnostic seals, geometric shapes, and human faces. No prayers or intentions are written on them, nor are they linked to any particular individual.

The Key of Solomon instructs that talismans be made at an astrologically significant time and on an appropriate day. Saturn talismans are to be made of lead; Jupiter, of tin; Mars, of iron; Sun, of gold; Venus, of copper; Moon, of silver; and Mercury, an amalgam of all the metals. They can also be made of exorcized virgin paper and drawn in colors appropriate to the planets.

Table 1 is a list of the colors of the planetary powers, according to the occultist Agrippa (who we will discuss later in this chapter). Although the text does not provide a consecration ritual, it states that incense should be burned during the pentacle's construction.

Table 1
The colors of the planetary powers, according to Agrippa.

Planet	Color
Saturn	Black
Jupiter	Blue
Mars	Red
Venus	Green
Mercury	Mixed colors
Moon	Silver
Sun	Gold or yellow

Many magicians use these pentacles as talismans, but this is not how they were intended to be used. Instead, the text shows the magician holding on to the pentacle when calling a spirit into physical manifestation during a ritual magic experiment.

We see pentacles used in similar ways in other magical systems, including the Heptameron, attributed to Peter de Abano, and Dr. John Dee in his Heptarchia. The idea is that by holding a pentacle with the relevant symbols on it, you control the being you are calling and can make the spirit do your bidding. In other words, a pentacle is a specialized talisman whose power is focused on assisting the magician in a particular ritual.

The Key of Solomon does mention that the pentacles can be carried about one's person to achieve a desired effect, but this would be to call upon any spirits to your aid quickly. It was a panic button that connected you directly to the spirits rather than a talisman as such.

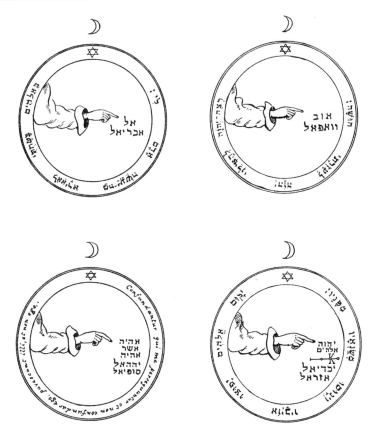

Figure 4. Luna pentacles from *The Key of Solomon*.

Magical Images on Talismans

During the Renaissance, the memory systems of ancient Rome were reactivated. These were originally designed to help people remember speeches. A person would imagine a scene, like a library, and place an image of what they wanted to remember at certain points in that library. For example, if you wanted to remember that Christopher Columbus rediscovered the Americas in 1492, you could imagine St. Christopher wearing a column on his head, driving a bus (Christopher Column bus), with an American flag draped over the front and the number 1492 on its destination window. As you recited your speech you could imagine yourself walking through that library, and the images would remind you of what to say next.

These images developed into a system of storing magical knowledge. If you wanted to remember the powers of Jupiter, you would visualize a crowned king wearing a purple robe, sitting on a cubic throne on the back of a huge crab, and holding an orb and scepter. You would see a person obediently bowing to him, and his face would be an expression of love. Above him would be the Hebrew letters אל (El), and on the orb would be the sign of Jupiter (♃). The person bowing would have the astrological symbols for Sagittarius (♐) and Aquarius (♒) on his back. To the king's left would be a devil, with goat's legs and hooves, holding the sign for Capricorn (♑). The devil would be threatening the king.

This would remind the occultist that Jupiter is attributed to Chesed, or Mercy, on the Cabbalistic Tree of Life, the divine name of which is El. Its symbols are the orb and rod of power. Jupiter is the power of love and authority. It rules Sagittarius and Aquarius, is exalted in Cancer, and is in fall in Capricorn.

This mental shorthand was considered to have a power all its own, which could be used in magical operations. Occultists call these "talismatic images," and they are the basis behind many different magical systems, including Tarot and ceremonial magic. When they are placed on a talisman, they attract all the powers that a magician associates with the image.

In his book *De vita Coelitus Comparanda*, Ficino includes some of these images and converts them from stylized drawings into Renaissance art. Another occultist,

Giordano Bruno, developed a list of these images for his book *The Secret of Shadows*. He was attempting to create a highly sophisticated system of images based on star magic. His images found their way into many different post-Renaissance magical cookbooks. Some of his magical images of astrological signs are watered-down versions of those of Agrippa, and clearly he, like many Renaissance magicians, owed a huge debt to this man.

Agrippa

The person who had perhaps the biggest influence on magic and talisman making during the Renaissance was Henry Cornelius Agrippa of Nettesheim.

Agrippa was born in 1486 in Cologne, Germany. He went to university in Cologne and Paris, where he developed an interest in magic. After a successful career in the military, he toured Europe acquiring more occult information before settling in Paris among a brotherhood of followers. By the age of twenty-three, he had gathered together most of his notes for what was to be his most significant work—*Occult Philosophy*. In 1509, he wrote the first draft and sent it to fellow occultist and friend Abbot Johannes Trithemius to be reviewed, but it was not until 1531 that it was first published. By that time Agrippa was much more Christian in his outlook. At the end of the book he even published a retraction of magic and praised the word of God.

Many have seen this as merely a front to get the book approved by the authorities. Attempts were certainly made by the Church to ban publication of the book, but they were largely unsuccessful. This was probably due to the fact that Agrippa's patron was Hermannus, the archbishop of Cologne.

The calm did not last long. Whipped into a frenzy by the Dominican monks, German Emperor Charles V sentenced Agrippa to death. But Agrippa escaped to France, where King Francis immediately flung him into prison. He was quickly released, but died soon afterward. He was forty-nine years old when he died, and, ironically, was buried by the Dominicans at one of their churches.[15]

Occult Philosophy is a three-volume encyclopedia of Renaissance esoteric knowledge. Much of the information on talismans created by the Cabbalists and the Jews is included, along with hierarchies of angels and demons, geomancy, magical alphabets, magic squares, and other techniques that will be described later in this book. Agrippa kindly provides talisman makers with information on how to key into powerful astrological influences with magical talismatic images. It is thanks to him that we know the hours when the forces of the planets are strongest. What Agrippa does not explain is how to use his system in a practical manner, which I will do in later chapters.

Table 2
Agrippa's talismatic images for the zodiac.

Astrological sign	Decan[16]	Image
Aries	First	A dark man clothed in white, well built, reddish eyes, strong and angry.
	Second	A woman dressed in red standing on a white cloth.
	Third	An angry, pale man with red hair, clothed in red, carrying a golden bracelet and a wooden staff.
Taurus	First	A naked man, an archer, and a farmer (who is sowing, ploughing), and building.
	Second	A naked man holding a key.
	Third	A man holding a snake and a dart.
Gemini	First	A man holding a rod and serving another.
	Second	A man holding a pipe, and another man digging the earth.
	Third	A man looking for a weapon and a fool holding a bird in his right hand and a pipe in his left hand.

Astrological sign	Decan	Image
Cancer	First	A virgin in fine clothes, crowned.
	Second	A well-dressed man; or a man and a woman sitting at a table, playing.
	Third	A man hunting with a lance and horn, calling forth his dogs.
Leo	First	A man riding on a lion.
	Second	A crowned head of an angry man, with his hands lifted up. A threatening man with a sword drawn in his right hand and a small shield in his left hand.
	Third	A young man, very sad and ill, who holds a whip.
Virgo	First	A virgin and a man casting seeds.
	Second	A dark man wearing furs, and a man with a brush of hair holding a bag.
	Third	An old, pale, deaf woman; or an old man leaning on a staff.
Libra	First	An angry man holding a pipe, and a man reading.
	Second	Two angry men and a well-dressed man sitting in a chair.
	Third	A violent man with a bow with a naked man before him, and another man holding bread in one hand and a cup in the other hand.
Scorpio	First	A well-dressed woman struck by two men.
	Second	A naked man and woman, and a man sitting on the ground. Two dogs bite one another.
	Third	A man on his knees while a woman hits him with a staff.

Astrological sign	Decan	Image
Sagittarius	First	A man in chainmail holding a naked sword.
	Second	A woman weeping, covered in clothes.
	Third	A golden man playing with a staff.
Capricorn	First	A man and woman carrying full bags.
	Second	Two women and a man looking at flying birds.
	Third	A chaste, wise, working woman, and a banker gathering money on a table.
Aquarius	First	A prudent man, and a woman spinning.
	Second	A man with a long beard.
	Third	A dark, angry man.
Pisces	First	A well-clothed man with a sack on his shoulder.
	Second	A pretty, well-dressed woman.
	Third	A naked man or youth with a beautiful young woman whose head is crowned with flowers.

Table 3
Agrippa's talismatic images of the planets.

Planet	Image
Saturn	An old man dressed in black, sitting on a high chair, his hands are above his head, and he holds either a fish or a sickle. Under his feet are a bunch of grapes and his head is covered with a black cloth.
Jupiter	A crowned man dressed in saffron-covered robes riding an eagle or a dragon. In his right hand is a dart and he is about to strike the eagle or dragon. Or a crowned naked man, who has his hands joined together and lifted up. He is sitting in a four-legged chair, which is carried by four winged boys. Or a man with the head of a lion, or ram and eagle's feet clothed in saffron-colored robes.

Planet	Image
Mars	An armed man riding on a lion carrying a naked sword in his right hand and a decapitated head in his left. Or a soldier armed and crowned with a long lance.
Sun	A crowned king clothed in saffron colors, sitting on a chair, holding a raven, with a globe under his feet. Or a woman crowned with fire, dancing and laughing while standing on a four-horsed chariot. In her right hand is a mirror, or shield, in her left. Leaning on her breast is a staff.
Venus	A woman with the head of a bird and the feet of an eagle, holding a dart in her hand. Or a naked young woman with her hair spread out, holding a mirror. There is a chain about her neck, and a handsome young man holds the chain with his left hand as he fixes her hair with his right hand. They look lovingly at each other, and a winged boy holding a sword or dart is about them.
Mercury	A handsome, bearded young man. In his left hand is a caduceus, and in his right is a dart. He has winged feet. Or a man sitting in a chair or riding on a peacock. He has eagle's feet and a crest on his head. In his left hand he holds a rooster or fire.
Moon	A man leaning on a staff, with a bird on his head and a flourishing tree before him. A horned woman riding a bull, a dragon with seven heads, or a crab. She has in her right hand a dart, and in her left a mirror. She is clothed in white or green and has on her head two snakes with horns joined together.

These images may seem strange to a modern mind, but they actually work on the deep levels of the unconscious. In many ways they are like dream images, and their meanings, although obtuse, can be understood through meditation.

The image should be pictured as clearly as possible in your imagination. Some magicians try to talk to the images; others just let their realizations about the images rise from their conscious to their unconscious minds. You should write down your realizations and mull them over until they are part of the language that your unconscious uses to talk to your conscious mind. Soon you may start having dreams where, say, you are talking to a man carrying a sword and riding a lion, and you will know that Martian forces are at play in your life.

This sort of work is necessary if you plan to put images on your talismans. In this book, we will be using these magical images to trigger unconscious associations during the talisman preparation process; however, there is no reason why they should not be placed directly onto talismans.

Francis Barrett

In 1801, when Britain was undergoing a Gothic revival, Francis Barrett published a manual of occult techniques called *The Magus*.

This book contains little that is original and, according to Francis King, is basically a translation of and paraphrases parts of Agrippa (including a book falsely attributed to Agrippa that dealt with black magic), Agrippa's mentor Johannes Trithemius, Peter de Albano's *Liber Experimentorium*, and John Heydon's *Harmony of the World*.[17]

In *The Magus*, we see the use of numbers and magic squares, Cabbalistic divine names, and the images of the planets (figure 5). What Barrett adds is a picture of six planetary talismans so that we know what they should look like. They are two disks of the appropriate metal joined by a line of cloth tape (probably in the appropriate color). Each disk has two fields, a center, and a circumference.

In the center of one of the disks is a magic square of the planet, the sign of the planet, and the appropriate Hebrew name of God. Around the circumference is the number of the spirit of the planet, another divine name, and the name of the intelligence of the planet.[18]

In the center of the second disk is the seal of the planet, the sign of the planet, and the sigil, or signature, of the intelligence.[19] Around the circumference of the second disk of the Saturn and Jupiter talisman are corrupted Latin phrases: "Accipe mihi Petitione O Domine" (Saturn), which approximates to "Accept my request O Lord,"

Figure 5. Magic seals or talismans from *The Magus* by Francis Barrett (London, 1801).

and "Confirmo O Deus Potentis simus" (Jupiter), which does not really make much sense but could be intended to mean something like "Make me strong and powerful O God." The other talismans lack a Latin prayer although it is possible that they were meant to have one that was left off the illustration.

Barrett also neglected to provide a talisman of the Moon. I can only assume that the reason for this is because, under his system, the names and magic squares were too long to fit into the illustrator's drawing.[20] The other problem was that six talismans, being an even number, was easier for the engraver to put neatly on the page than the complete set of seven talismans.

For the sake of completeness, figure 6 illustrates what Barrett's talisman of the Moon would have looked like alongside the original engraving. I have used the Hebrew lettering he suggests.[21]

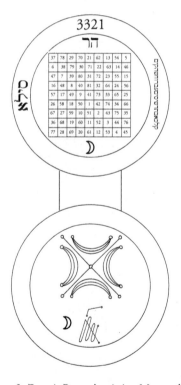

Figure 6. Francis Barrett's missing Moon talisman.

Barrett included magical images of the planets, which are similar to those provided by Agrippa, but for some reason did not include them in his final talismans. Perhaps once again it was the limitations of his illustrator who, while capable of performing great feats in the rest of the book, did not consider it possible to place an image of the planets in such a tiny space.

Barrett also mentions techniques for making pentacles similar to those in *The Key of Solomon*. These he describes as "certain holy signs and characters which, preserving us from evil chances and events, helping and assisting us to bind, exterminate and drive away evil spirits and reconciling them to us."[22]

The pentacles contain the "characters of good spirits, sacred pictures of holy letters or revelations with apt and proper versicles which are composed of geometric figures."[23] Although this sounds like he is describing his talismans, there are some differences. The pentacles are not planetary and are focused on the purpose of a particular ritual.

Pentacles are circular and have an appropriate name of God around the circumference. "If a pentacle were be made to gain victory or revenge against one's enemies, a figure might be taken out of the second book of the Maccabees. That is to say, a hand holding a golden sword drawn, about which let there be written the verse 'take the holy sword, the gift of God, where with thou shall slay the adversaries of my people Israel.'"[24]

Barrett adds that around this image you would draw an angular figure according to the rule of numbers. In other words, for his revenge talisman you would draw a pentagon, which represents the number five, which is attributed to Mars. This you would hold in your hands when you performed your ritual of revenge.

While Barrett was a figure of fun in his personal life (being obsessed with ballooning—the few historical references we have of him are his failed attempts to get off the ground), his book *The Magus* was a significant influence on most of the magical orders that came after him—including the Esoteric Order of the Golden Dawn.[25]

The Esoteric Order of the Golden Dawn

Founded in 1888 by Freemasons, the Esoteric Order of the Golden Dawn was crucial in the development of the Western magical tradition. There are very few magical organizations that do not have some link with the Golden Dawn or feature some of its techniques. What it did was take many magical and esoteric systems and place them under a single umbrella, in a similar way to what Barrett did, but on a much larger scale. The order lasted until the turn of the century, when it broke into factions: the Stella Matertina, the Alpha Et Omega, and a mystical version called the Fellowship of the Rosy Cross. Of these, the Stella Matertina existed in England until 1972 and in New Zealand until 1979. The Golden Dawn's approach to talismans was similar to Barrett; however, it added the concept of Cabbalah and color to the magical mix.

The Cabbalistic diagram, the Tree of Life, shows ten divisions of God. Each of these divisions, or Sepharoth, represents aspects of the divine. These are the Crown (Kether), Wisdom (Chockmah), Understanding (Binah), Mercy (Chesed), Justice (Geburah), Beauty (Tiphareth), Victory (Netzach), Splendor (Hod), Foundation (Yesod), and the Kingdom (Malkuth). A tree could be drawn for each of the four levels or worlds and was used as a cataloging system for all esoteric knowledge.

The first Tree contains the names of God, the second the names of the archangels, the third the names of the choir of angels, and the fourth the physical expression of the four worlds. Tiphareth thus has the divine name YHVH Eloah Ve Daath, אלוה ודעת יהוה, which means "God of Knowledge." On the second level, it has the archangel Raphael, רפאל, or "God has Healed." On the third level, it has the Melekim, מיכים, which means "messengers"; they provide stability and balance, healing and life. On the last level is the physical expression of all these forces—the Sun.[26]

In the higher levels of the Golden Dawn, color was used to achieve magical effects. The technique was quite simple; each of the four Cabbalistic levels had a color system. These were called the King, Queen, Prince, and Princess scales. There were four different Trees of Life painted in these scales: Chesed in the King scale would be violet, in the Queen scale it would be blue, in the Emperor scale it would be purple, and in the Empress scale it would be azure flecked with gold.

These colors were believed to attract magical forces. This effect was further enhanced by writing magical names, sigils, and so on, in a complementary color, which jazzes the eyes so much that it gives the appearance that the lettering is alive. The Golden Dawn called this effect "flashing colors." They also developed tablets of flashing colors that could trap planetary energy so that it could be put into a talisman or used in other magical operations.

The Golden Dawn used its elaborate initiation system to develop rituals that empowered the talismans. They believed that as their initiation system brought a candidate (who was spiritually dead) to life, it could also be used to bring a physical object to life.

There is no doubt that, within the Golden Dawn, talisman making was at its most elaborate. These were truly beautiful and effective magical items. They applied this technique to all their magical equipment, from swords to magical wands, thus enhancing all their rites with the powers of many talismans.

As the Golden Dawn influence started to wane, though, so, too, did interest in talismans. The successors to the Golden Dawn sought less complicated methods of building talismans.

Successors to the Golden Dawn

The research into talisman development all but died out for many years within the main esoteric Orders, who tended either to make talismans according to the Golden Dawn formula, or just left them alone. Dion Fortune, for example, did not mention talismans in any of her teachings, and it does not seem that they were taught within her school, the Fraternity of Inner Light.

After long research at the British Library, Madeline Mountalban, an associate of Aleister Crowley, gathered together an eclectic system of angel magic that featured the use of talismans. Generally, Montalban's system involved writing letters to the main archangels in one of two alphabets (which were taken from Agrippa), the Passing the River and the Theban scripts.[27] These letters to the seven archangels were burnt when the task had been completed.

Talismans in the Montalban system were easy to make and consecrate. For example, one talisman, which was supposed to protect you from an enemy, simply required the magician to draw one of the Abramelin squares on a piece of paper in red ink (figure 7).

M	E	B	H	A	E	R
E	L	I	A	I	L	E
B	I	K	O	S	I	A
H	A	O	R	O	A	H
A	I	S	O	K	I	B
E	L	I	A	I	L	E
R	E	A	H	B	E	M

Figure 7. Montalban protection talisman.

The square had to be written on a Tuesday while a red candle was burned. Instead of using English letters, the square was to be written in the Passing of the Rivers script.

After the talisman had been completed, the candle was extinguished in a bowl of water and had to be stored in a warm place. When your enemy's plans had been thwarted and they had left you alone, the talisman could be safely destroyed.

The simplicity of this magic act belies how difficult it is. As the square is created there is a certain amount of magical power, which makes it easy to make a mistake in drawing the figures.

Montalban's system proved that talismans did not have to be complex to be effective. What was important was an inner connection to the beings called. It reminded magicians that although talisman magic often featured elaborate sigils, names of power, and colors, at the end of the day they could all be replaced by an unshakeable faith in the system. It is Montalban's system that has been adopted by many Alexandrian Wiccan covens.

What Montalban and those who succeeded her also developed was a system of testing whether a talisman was working. They did this by requesting the beings that empowered the talisman to give signs that they were working on it. These are called "checks on earth" or "signs following." For example, the angel of Mars, Sachiel, would acknowledge that a request to him was positively received by arranging for the magician to receive a knife, or see knives falling to the ground, or a shower of sparks.

Another modern influence on talisman making was the British grotesque surrealist artist A. O. Spare. In his attempts to draw up a simple magical system, which he named *Zos*, Spare, who was influenced by Crowley, developed what he called *alphabetic sigils*. This involved writing a simple sentence expressing what you wanted. The letters in the sentence would be crossed out so that nothing was repeated, and the letters that were left would be combined to make a magic sigil.

Spare would have you stare at the sigil for a few moments before forgetting about it and letting its work be done; however, sigils like these have been used on modern talismans either to express an intention or to represent the person for whom it is designed.

Now, having discussed talismans and their uses in the past, it is now time to look at the key teachings behind creating talismans of power of your own.

---

1. The term *shaman*, strictly speaking, refers to the spiritual leaders of Siberian tribes; however, in modern times it has come to define the same role in most cultures. *Shaman* is more politically correct than the term *witch doctor*.

2. The *world tree* is the primal tree from which all life springs forth. Shamanic journeys were often described as climbing this tree, or descending to its roots.

3. The permafrost of Siberia makes the ground too hard to bury a person or object in, so the dead were hung in trees.

4. See T. G. H. James, *Introduction to Ancient Egypt* (London: British Museum Press, 1979), 135. This is a guide to the British Museum's collection.

5. See *The Book of the Dead*, translated by E. A. Wallis Budge (New York, NY: Dover Publications, 1967) 88.

6. See Gideon Bohak, "Aggressive Magic." The Michigan Society of Fellows and Department of Classical Studies, 1996 Exhibition. At the time of writing this book, the website address for this page was www.hti.umich/exhibit/magic.

7. See David G. Martinez, "PMich 757: A Greek Love Charm from Egypt," Ann Arbor, 1991. At the time of writing this book, this charm could be found in full at www.hti.umich/exhibit/magic.

8. See T. Schrire, *Hebrew Amulets* (London: Routledge & Kegan Paul, 1966).

9. See John Matthews, *The Grail Seeker's Companion* (Wellingborough: Aquarian, 1984) 58.

10. See T. Schrire, *Hebrew Amulets* (London: Routledge & Kegan Paul, 1966) 14.

11. Although it is called the seventy-two-lettered name of God, Shem Hameforash actually has 216 letters. These are arranged in seventy-two syllables of three letters each.

12. See T. Schrire, *Hebrew Amulets* (London: Routledge & Kegan Paul, 1966).

13. Psalm 91:11 reads, "For he shall give his angels charge over thee, to keep thee in thy ways."

14. The meaning of Exodus 11:8 is a little obscure. The verse reads, "And all these thy servants shall come unto me and bow themselves down unto me, saying Get thee out and all the people that follow thee: and after that I will go out. And he went from Pharaoh in a great anger." This is possibly a reference to the birthing process.

15. For a more detailed biography of Agrippa and a very readable translation of his work, see Henry Cornelius Agrippa, *Three Books of Occult Philosophy,* ed. Donald Tyson (Saint Paul, MN: Llewellyn Publishing, 1995).

16. The twelve signs of the zodiac are divided into three "decans," which are ten-degree sections of each sign. In traditional astrology, these are ruled by each of the planets in what is called the Chaldean order. In modern astrology, each sign takes the ruler of the triplicity in order; so, for example, the first decan of Aries is ruled by Mars, the second decan by the Sun, and the third decan by Jupiter.

17. See Francis King, *The Flying Sorcerer* (Mandrake Press, 1986) 18.

18. I will be explaining the difference between archangels, angels, spirits, and intelligences in chapter 4.

19. This is taken from the magic square. We will discuss magic squares in chapter 6.

20. According to Barrett, the intelligence of the intelligences of the Moon is Malcha betharsisim hed beruah schehalim. His number was 3321. The magic square, which is nine by nine squares, was also too big for the center (the engraver seemed to have only just fitted in the eight by eight squares of Mercury), particularly as it would have had to share the space with the divine name Elim and the ☽ sign for the Moon.

21. See Francis Barrett, *The Magus* (York Beach, ME: Weiser, 2000) 147.

22. Ibid., 80.

23. Ibid.

24. Ibid., 81.

25. See Francis King, *The Flying Sorcerer* (Mandrake Press, 1986).

26. We will examine the Tree of Life and the Cabbalah in chapter 3.

27. We will examine Montalban's system in chapter 4.

3

Names of Power

In this chapter we are going to look at how to tap into the unlimited energy of the universe to empower your talismans. We will also examine how divine names and images of the gods can be used to create different effects.

Everyone has a divine part of himself or herself, a fragment that passes from incarnation to incarnation, learning and perfecting its true essence. Since this divine self is part of an indivisible infinite wholeness, we are connected to the infinite universe.

The difference between powerful and mediocre magicians is the degree of unity they have with their divine natures. Successful magicians achieve miracles in their magic because, for a brief instant, they allow this divine aspect to express itself through their limited personalities. As all of creation responds to its creator, so the universe heeds the voice of the magician.

How is it possible to key into this divine self? Well, the answer is "Slowly!" It is a gradual process that takes lifetimes to master. You identify yourself with the divine until you achieve the realization of your true nature. Magicians spend their lives rehearsing for this realization *as if it were already so*.

While I may not yet have the powers of the universe at my fingertips, sometimes, thanks to the power of ritual, I do have this power for a moment. When the ritual brings about the desired effect, I am one step closer to the grand realization.

Magicians also use the power of forms and names. The Eastern mystery traditions and the mystics achieve enlightenment by rejecting all gods and forms of gods as an illusion. They push aside these illusions as a way of seeing the real God behind them. On the other hand, the Western magician, while still acknowledging that images and gods are ultimately illusions, uses them as rungs in a ladder, gradually ascending the levels until they are no longer needed. Images of gods and divine names are thus like buses that magicians catch to take them to this divine realization.

When divine names or images are placed on a talisman, they represent the divine power that the magician is tapping into to achieve the correct effect.

As we discussed in chapter 2, the Hebrews and the Egyptians considered writing a way of capturing tremendous amounts of divine power.

In Hebrew, each letter was considered to be holy and was believed to have come from the mouth of God. Each letter had an image and a number associated with it.

Table 4
Images and numbers associated with Hebrew letters.

Name	Hebrew Letter	Meaning	Numeric value
Aleph	א	Ox	1
Beth	ב	House	2
Gimel	ג	Camel	3
Daleth	ד	Door	4
He	ה	Window	5
Vau	ו	Nail	6
Zayin	ז	Sword	7
Cheth	ח	Boundary	8
Teth	ט	Snake	9
Yod	י	Hand	10
Kaph	כ	Fist	20
Lamed	ל	Ox Goad	30
Mem	מ	Water	40
Nun	נ	Fish	50

Name	Hebrew Letter	Meaning	Numeric value
Samekh	ס	Prop	60
Ayin	ע	Eye	70
Pe	פ	Mouth	80
Tzaddi	צ	Fish Hook	90
Qoph	ק	Back of the Head	100
Resh	ר	Face	200
Shin	ש	Tooth	300
Tau	ת	Cross	400

When we see a Hebrew name of power, we have a number and a series of images that we can associate with it that give clues about its meaning.

Take, for example, the divine name El, which is made from the letters אל. This means we have Aleph the Ox and Lamed the Ox Goad. As oxen were the driving force for the development of agriculture, they are symbolic of the evolution of life. In an agricultural society, the more oxen you owned, the greater amount of power you had, so they are also a symbol of power. An ox goad is a force that drives the oxen by threatening them with pain if they do not do the drover's bidding; therefore, the ox goad is a symbol of law. The name El is thus the divine power in motion working through the laws of life.

By adding together the numbers of these letters, we can find associations between these words and others. This is called *Gematria*, and the meanings that are usually unlocked are generally esoteric. For example, the letters in the name El come to a combined total of thirty-one. If you reduce this number further by adding the three and the one, you get four, which indicates a link between the divine name El and the letter Daleth. It suggests that the divine forces represented by El are a doorway or passage between what the Supreme Being is thinking and the world of form.

The interesting part of this technique is that it can be used to derive new meanings from the Bible and explains why whole sections of the Old Testament are dedicated to seemingly meaningless measurements and long genealogies.

It can be taken too far, though, as Aleister Crowley jokingly pointed out by interpreting nursery rhymes using Cabbalistic techniques including Gematria. Crowley's joke was a little more amusing than the two-hour lecture based on the Gematria of Joshua 12:5 that I once had to endure.[1] This lecture featured mental gymnastics and number and letter play and was about as spiritually useful as staring at a brick for the same length of time.

So, what divine names should be used? Most Western occultists use a symbol called the Tree of Life.

The Tree of Life

The Tree of Life is a road map for enlightenment that is used in the Jewish mystical system called the Cabbalah (figure 8). It can also be used like a mental filing cabinet in which to catalogue all esoteric knowledge. Because the Cabbalah was so effective, Christian magicians hijacked it during the Renaissance and developed it along their own lines. This is how Cabbalah works:

Imagine you are an infinite, unknowable God who wants to understand itself. Your first realization is that you are unknowable and without limits and seem to be made up of energy. The problem with being limitless is that you can't possibly encompass all you really are. The only way is to restrict yourself within time and space.

You create a point of yourself that contains everything you are. The Cabbalists called this point *Kether*, which means "the Crown." Into it is poured as much of the consciousness of the Supreme Being as possible. The Cabbalists called this aspect of God Eheieh, אהיה, which means "I am." In other words, God allowed part of itself to become aware.

But that was not enough. When you want to look at yourself, you use a mirror. When you, the god, look in the mirror, your reflection is called *Chockmah*, which means "Wisdom." The divine name for this sphere is Yah יה.

This Wisdom is a blind force, and there is nothing to contain it and no way to understand yourself; so from Wisdom is created *Binah*, or "Understanding." The divine name of this sphere is Tetragrammaton Elohim, יהוה אלהים, which means literally "Lord God"; however, because the word Elohim is a feminine noun with a masculine ending, it is often seen as the feminine or passive side of God. This is the perfect counterpart to *Chockmah*, the male or positive side of God.

Continuing to play the part of God, you are now aware, looking into a mirror, and using force and form to create the universe—much in the same way that you meditate using pictures or daydreams.

The next thing you need to develop is the ability to create and destroy your images. The creative side is called *Chesed*, or "Mercy," and the destructive side is called *Geburah*, which means "Severity." The Cabbalists say that these two forces balance each other perfectly. The divine name for the creative aspect is *El*, אל, which means "God," while the destructive side is *Elohim Gibor*, אלהים גבור, which means "the God of Battles."

Next, you know you are going to have to start building things out of yourself and move closer to your creation if you are to experience it properly, so you create a sphere called *Tiphareth*, or "Beauty." This is because your creation will have you at its heart. The divine name for this sphere is YHVH Eloah ve-Daath, אלוה ודעת יהוה, which means "Lord God of Knowledge." It is through this aspect of God that the universe's creation is controlled.

So far, you have not yet created anything. You are still the same single entity. So next you divide yourself into the myriad energies from which your creation will be formed. This phase is called *Netzach*, or "Victory," and the divine name for God at this point is YHVH Tzaboath or יהוה צבאות, which means "Lord of Hosts." In other words, YHVH Tzaboath is the single ruler who has become expressed through many different things.

None of these forces have forms, however, so you have to allow part of yourself to have a multitude of shapes. This great form-building exercise is called *Hod*, or "Splendor," and the name of God at this point is Elohim Tzabaoth, אלהים צבאות, which literally means "God of Hosts." This is the Supreme Being who is expressed through many.

These forms that have been created at Hod and Netzach lack the substance required to form the universe as we know it. You need to build a more solid frame for the universe and move deeper into what we call *physicality*, so you create another divine sphere called *Yesod*, which means "Foundation" and literally underpins the physical universe. God at this point has the divine name Shaddai El Chai, שדי אל חי, which means "Almighty Living God."

Finally, with the processes and foundations built, you create your universe. This material plane is called *Malkuth*, which means "Kingdom," and the divine name for God at this point is Adonai Ha Aretz, אדני הארץ, which means "Lord of the Earth."

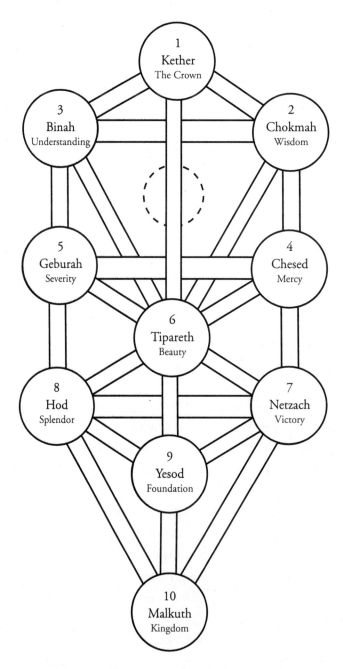

Figure 8. The Tree of Life.

The Tree of Life is a graphic representation of this process.

In addition to divine names, magicians and Cabbalists attribute different aspects of creation to different spheres on the Tree of Life. Perhaps the most important of these attributions for talisman makers is the allocation of the planets to the different spheres.

Table 5
Cabbalistic attributions to the planets.

Name of Sphere	Divine Name	Planetary force
Kether	Eheieh	The Primum Mobile
Chockmah	YHVH	The Zodiac
Binah	YHVH	Elohim Saturn
Chesed	El	Jupiter
Geburah	Elohim Gibor	Mars
Tiphareth	YHVH Eloah ve-Daath	Sun
Netzach	YHVH Tzaboath	Venus
Hod	Elohim Tzaboath	Mercury
Yesod	Shaddai El Chai	Moon
Malkuth	Adonai Ha Aretz	The four elements and the world

So, if we were building a talisman to attract the powers of Venus, we would use the divine name YHVH Tzaboath in our talisman.

We can also gauge some of the powers of each sphere by the sort of planets that are attributed to them. Chesed, for example has the expansive, creative, and ruling tendencies that astrologers associate with Jupiter, and Hod has all the intellectual, form-building tendencies we associate with Mercury.

Paths, which are halfway houses between these different aspects of God, connect the spheres on the Tree of Life. There are twenty-two of these paths, one for each of the Hebrew letters. The path between Kether and Chockmah is thus attributed to the Hebrew letter Aleph, א, and the path between Malkuth and Yesod is attributed to the Hebrew letter Tau, ת.

To those that have no experience with magic or Cabbalah, these names will not have much meaning. They will seem unpronounceable and divorced from the divine forces that they represent. To be effective, the magician has to make a contact with that divine force and hold a concept of it.

This is achieved over time, but there are exercises that can help speed up the process. The easiest is a technique called "Building the Tree of Life in the Aura."[2] Many modern occultists will recognize this exercise as an extension of the Middle Pillar that was popularized by Israel Regardie. Ideally, it should be performed every day for two weeks before attempting to make a talisman. Another little ritual called the Cabbalistic Cross should be performed first.

The Cabbalistic Cross

The Cabbalistic Cross is a ritual visualization exercise that balances energy and seals the electromagnetic shell around your body, which is known as the aura. It places you under the protection of divine forces and, with regular use, strengthens the aura. It is performed before and after a ritual to harmonize the energy that you have received in your meditation work.

Standing upright, close your eyes and visualize a bright white ball of light above you. This is the highest expression of the power of God of which you are capable of conceiving at this time. Visualize it until you can almost feel its warmth on the top of your head. Visualize it beginning to spin.

Say the Hebrew word ATAH [Ah-tah], which means "thou art." Touch your forehead with the fingertips of your right hand and see a line of light from the white sphere travel down to where your fingers connect with your forehead.

Draw your fingers in a straight line down the center of your torso to your breast. See the light follow your fingers and carry on down your body toward a white sphere just below and including your feet. As the light pours into this sphere, see it glow, brighten, and spin.

Say the Hebrew word MALKUTH [Mahl-kooth], which means "the Kingdom."

Tap your right shoulder and see a white sphere start to spin. Say the Hebrew words VE GEBORAH [Ve-ge-boor-ah], which mean "and the Power."

Draw another line of white across your body to your left shoulder and visualize another sphere of bright light starting to spin.

Say the Hebrew words VE GEDULAH [Ve Ge doo-lah], which mean "and the Glory."

Now bring your hands together over your heart where the lines of light meet. Hold your hands as if you were praying.

Say the Hebrew words LA OLAM [lay-oh-lam], which mean "forever, Amen [ah-men]."

See white light expand from your heart until your entire body is enclosed in a sphere of white light.

See yourself as a cross of light-tipped with glowing spheres, and see your aura filled with white light.

Building the Tree of Life in the Aura

Your will need to know how to vibrate a divine name in order to perform this exercise. When you vibrate a divine name, you take a deep breath; push the sound to the roof of your mouth while contracting your throat. When the sound vibrates, you will feel it deep within your throat and nose. The best place to experiment with this is in the bath where the acoustics will help you find the right pitch. Vibration is loud, so it is best to practice when there is no one else at home.

As you vibrate each divine name, you will have a different feeling with each one. Note what these feelings are and, preferably, write them down. These are the energies of the divine names, and the more you use them the more familiar you will become with them. You will recognize if a talisman is vibrating to a particular energy and will know if a ritual dedicated to that name is working correctly.

Sit poised on a straight-backed chair. Your chin should be slightly inclined toward your chest so that your neck is straight. Your thighs should be horizontal, your calves vertical, and your feet in line with your hips and firmly planted on the floor.

Your hands should be resting in your lap. This posture allows the forces contacted in the meditation to flow freely.

The ability to relax at will is crucial for any occult work. When seated in the meditation position, focus on your feet, tense the muscles in your feet for about three seconds, and then allow them to relax.

Focus on the calves of your legs; tense and then relax them. Continue this process throughout the entire body. Don't forget your facial muscles!

Next, you should regulate your breathing. Altered breathing patterns build up subtle changes within the bloodstream and enhance meditation and ritual work.

You should breathe from your diaphragm, which is situated below the rib cage in the abdomen. It is unnecessary to pull in the breath or force anything—just push out the diaphragm and the rib cage will expand and air will rush into your lungs. Contracting your lungs will push out the old air. You should not hear anything. If you hear sound, then you are forcing the process too much. The solution to this is to slow down.

The breath cycle begins as you empty your lungs and then inhale deeply for a count of four. Hold your breath for a count of two; exhale completely for a count of four; maintain your exhaled breath for a count of two; then inhale to a count of four. The counting should be your own, matched to your own lung capacity.

Once you are completely relaxed, this breath cycle should be established consciously for at least six full cycles. You may then move on to the next stage—the formation of the Tree in the aura.

Take a deep breath and visualize the white ball of light above your head. See it expand and begin to spin. Vibrate the divine name Eheieh [eh-hey-yay]. Do this six times.

Imagine the light flowing down to a white ball of light at the nape of your neck. See it expand and begin to spin. Vibrate the divine name YHVH Elohim [Yod-hey-vav-hey El-oh-heem]. Do this six times.

Imagine the light flowing down to a white ball of light near your heart. See it expand and begin to spin. Vibrate the divine name YHVH Eloah Va-Daath [Yod-hey-vav-hey El-oh-ah ve-Dah-arth]. Do this six times.

Imagine the light flowing down to a white ball of light near your groin. See it expand and begin to spin. Vibrate the divine name Shaddai El-Chai [Sha-dye El-Chai]. Do this six times.

Imagine the light flowing down to a white ball of light at your feet. See it expand and begin to spin. Vibrate the divine name Adonai-Ha-Aretz [ah-doe-nye-ha aretz]. Do this six times.

Shift your concentration to the crown sphere at the top of your head. Vibrate Eheieh [eh-hey-yay] again. Imagine the light flowing down to a white ball of light on the right side of your head. See it expand and begin to spin. Vibrate the divine name Yah. Do this six times.

Now see the light move across to a sphere on the left side of your head. See it expand and begin to spin. Vibrate the divine name YHVH Elohim [Yod-hay-vav-hay El-oh-heem]. Do this six times.

See the light move across to a sphere on your right shoulder, passing through the throat center, which illuminates as the light passes through it. See the sphere begin to spin. Vibrate the divine name El [Ee-el] Do this six times.

See the light move across to a sphere on your left shoulder. See it expand and begin to spin. Vibrate the divine name Elohim Gibor [El-oh-heem Gib-oor]. Do this six times.

Now see the light move across to a sphere on your right hip, passing through the heart center, which lights up as the light passes through it. See the sphere on your left hip expand and begin to spin. Vibrate the divine name YHVH Tzaboath [Yod-hey-vav-hey Zar-Bo-oth]. Do this six times.

See the light move across to a sphere on your left hip. See the sphere expand and begin to spin. Vibrate the divine name Elohim Tzaboath [El-oh-heem Zar-Bo-oth]. Do this six times.

Now see the light passing to the groin center, which lights up, and then into the earth center at your feet. Vibrate the divine name Adonai-Ha-Aretz [ah-doe-nye-ha aretz] again. Do this six times.

Allow the light to begin to encircle your aura. Begin on your left side at about the same distance as your outstretched arm. Let it flow over your head to your right side, then under your feet to your left side. Continue to do this for about a minute.

When the light reaches the top of your head, change its direction to flow down your front to your feet, then under your feet to your back, then up your back to the top of your head. Continue to do this for a while.

When the light reaches your feet, breathe out and then, as you breathe in, draw the light up your spine to the sphere of life above your head. Breathe out and let this center explode with white light that showers through your aura, cleaning and purifying it. Allow the light to gather at your feet. Repeat the process at least ten times.

Finish with a Cabbalistic Cross.

I recommend that you complete your Tree of Life energy session with a period of meditation on one of the divine names. Take each letter of a name and meditate on what they mean. Let the images form in your mind.

If you choose to meditate on the name Yesod, which is Shaddai El Chai, אל חי שדי, make up a little story in your head about the letters. The cast of your story would be a tooth, two doors, two hands, and an ox goad. It may be a little hard at first, but once your unconscious mind gets in on the act, you will start to gain some surprising insights. Think of the associations made for each of these letters. A tooth, for example, is the hardest part of the human body. Teeth assist in the breaking down of food so the body can use it. A door is a gateway to another place. From those two letters alone we have the idea of something that is solid and eternal that converts energy from one thing to another and moves through many different dimensions. Remember that the goal will to be to find out more about the Supreme Being as it manifests as the "foundation of the world" and particularly as the Moon.

Later, when you inscribe one of these divine names on your talisman, you will be making a statement about what you actually know about that particular god.

Bible Verses

As we discussed in chapter 2, Bible verses can bestow talismans with divine power. They become like divine names in their own right and are treated as such by their position on the talisman.

A list of divine names taken from Bible verses and designed for talismanic purposes is shown in table 6. Alongside traditional names, I have included some names taken from Bible verses associated with particular functions. For example, a talisman to find calm in a period of stress would use Psalm 62, verses 1 and 2: "My soul finds rest in Elohim alone: my salvation comes only from him. He is my rock and my salvation. He is my fortress. I shall never be shaken."[3]

To convert this verse into a name of power, you would consult an interlinear Hebrew-English Bible and take the first letter of each word of the verse; or, if it were a long passage, the letter from the beginning and end of each verse. The name should be written backward. In this case, we have the name ראלמשעהאימנדאאא.

Table 6 is a list of the planets and various talismanic uses associated with each planet. Under each talismanic use, I have listed some corresponding divine names and the Bible verses from which they come.

Some of these divine names are traditional and their meanings are often obscure; modern magicians use the others. These have been tested and used successfully on talismans, however ultimately it will be up to you to find your own and see if they are successful.

Table 6
Hebrew notarikon taken from Bible verses.

Sun
Healing.
Numbers 12:13 ומאילאנרנל

To cure sterility.
Deuteronomy 7:12 ועתאההוואויאנלווו

Moon
To understand the secrets of dreams and the unconscious.
Deuteronomy 29:29 הלאוההלאכההכעיכו[4]

Aid in childbirth.
Genesis 21:1 ופאשכאוילכר

To guard against obsession and illusions.

Exodus 15:16 תעאובזיכעיעיעוקבות

To improve one's memory.

Proverbs 16:1 למלומלרובזארכ

Isaiah 26:1 למלומל

To end worry.

Psalm 37 יכמוככליכילייירכתתיחשאשזוואלכמהדייולגאוייבכעא

For happiness and to cure depression.

Psalm 30:11 שושפללמה

Mercury

To aid in writing.

Psalms 45:3 (part) מסע

For a good singing voice.

Exodus 15:1 אימויאהלולאלאלכנגסורב

To win an intellectual argument.

Deuteronomy 32:11–12 ההוואהאפיכלתכא

To have total knowledge of a school subject.

Ezekiel 3:3 בתותאהה

To aid in study.

Psalms 119:49 זבלעאי

To preserve someone from lies or to cure a liar.

Psalms 34:13 ממומלנ

Safety during travel.

Numbers 10:35 ובהומקיואוממ

Venus

To find one's life partner.

Genesis 2:22–23 ילמכאילמומעזהוראוהאולהמלאאהעותבומאהעתאיו

Genesis 24:40 אומלאווואמגלהאיאו

For sexual happiness between partners.
Genesis 2:24–25 יווהעשואלובואואאאיכע

Mars

Success in conflict.
Exodus 15:9 אאאאאשתדנאהתי
Exodus 15:7 ונתקתחיכ

To counteract a psychic attack.
Exodus 23:22 אממכרל
Numbers 11:12 ההאכההאאי
Isaiah 41:24 האמומהיב
Exodus 33:23 ואכואאולי

To create fear in your enemies.
Exodus 15:15 אנאאאמידנכיכ

Protection against fire.
Numbers 11:2 והאמומאיווה

Protection against theft.
Psalms 97:2 עוסעומכ

Protection from enemies.
Psalms 3 לשלעקילקרוסרעי

General protection.
Psalms 16:1 בחכאש

To cause an enemy's attack to rebound upon him or her.
Psalms 34:21 יצוררת[5]

Jupiter

For general success.
Genesis 39:2 ואאיואמובאה
Numbers 26:46 ובאש

To turn defeat into success.

Genesis 41:14 ופאיומהוושואפ

For a profitable business.

Genesis 31:42 לאאאאויהלכערש

For peace between enemies.

Psalms 46:9 בעחוייקהקעממ[6]

Saturn

For a happy home.

Genesis 37:1 ויבמאבכ

Genesis 47:27 ויבמבגובוומ

To improve understanding of a problem or life.

Joshua 1:4 מודוהודההגפ

---

1. Joshua 12:5 reads, "And they all reigned in Mount Hermon and in Salcah and in all Bashan unto the border of the Geshurites and the Maachathites and half Gilead the border of the Sihon king of Hesbon."
2. This is often called the *Middle Pillar exercise*.
3. Remember that *Elohim* is a feminine version of *God*, so legitimately *he* could be replaced with *she* in this verse.
4. There is a one-verse discrepancy between the Hebrew and the English numbering of this chapter. The English verse is 29, and the Hebrew verse is 28.
5. There is a one-verse discrepancy between the English and the Hebrew verse numbering. The English verse is 21, and the Hebrew verse is 20.
6. There is a one-verse discrepancy between the Hebrew and the English numbering of this chapter. The English verse is 9, and the Hebrew verse is 10.

4

Neo-Pagan Talismans

The names of power we examined in the previous chapter are from the Jewish/Cabbalistic tradition. We will build on this information later to create more complex talismans within the Western magical tradition; however, within Western magic there are deities that belong to the so-called "Pagan" or "Neo-Pagan" tradition that also can be used for making talismans.

Pagan was a term coined in the Middle Ages for those who lived in the countryside. Christianity was a religion of the towns and cities, and rural people still held onto traditions dating back to non-Christian civilizations.

There has been a resurgence of interest in Pagan religions since the 1960s. Many people are returning to the old gods again in an attempt to find a spiritual purity that they feel has deserted the Christian tradition. They are worshipping their gods and goddesses in a different way from their ancient ancestors.

Ironically, it was Christianity that bought religion closer to the masses by allowing "ordinary" people to develop a personal relationship with God by taking part in Christian rituals. Now, Neo-Pagans have returned to their original gods and goddesses with this lesson learned, placing a modern gloss on the old traditions.

Ancient Pagan practice was simple. Each geographic location had its own pantheon, legends, heroes, and names. Generally, priests and priestesses represented them. People who wanted their gods to intervene in their lives, or to know the future, would seek out a priest who would approach the deity on their behalf.

Most Pagans deal with their deities directly. Their gods and goddesses are working within them and within their environment and are seen as having a relationship with the worshipper.

Some Neo-Pagans worship a pantheon of individual gods and goddesses. Others worship an archetypal "goddess" who has three aspects—maiden, mother, and crone; and a god, who sometimes has a subsidiary role.

There are also modern Pagans who are interested in recreating the ancient religions of Denmark, Egypt, Germany, Greece, and Mesopotamia.

In recreating a Pagan approach to making and consecrating talismans, I have tried to give a magical experience of the different divinities so that talisman making can be a way for Neo-Pagans and Wiccans to interact with their gods and goddesses.

It is possible for non-Pagans to use this system, too, provided that they can acknowledge that Pagan deities are essentially masks of the One Deity. Most Neo-Pagans do not have to make this intellectual leap and, by adopting a pantheistic approach, accept that they are just looking at one face of a bigger whole.

A Pagan Approach

To recreate a form of Pagan practice, you need to have developed a relationship with a god or goddess in a particular pantheon. This deity is your Patron and is often the main god you will work with during your lifetime.

A Patron can be seen as a friend, teacher, guide, helper, or religious inspiration. Since each deity has a particular energy, it is likely that your life will be colored by the particular force of that energy. For example, people with Venus as their Patron deity are often loving, artistic types, with a streak of mischief and vanity.

Finding your Patron is a quest in itself. It is won by experience and trying out the different energies to find a deity that suits you. A good place to start might be to consider your astrological Sun sign. The sign Leo, for example, is ruled by the Sun, so someone with a Leo Sun and find a Patron god in Apollo, Ra, Lugh, or Frey. Aries is ruled by Mars, so someone with an Aries Sun might find a Patron in Ares, Thor, Bran, or Horus.

In addition to your Patron, you will have a teaching deity and another god or goddess to whom you might appeal for a particular need. These deities will have to be approached through your Patron and are only in your life for a period of time.

Later in this chapter, I will list of each of the Pagan deities in the major pantheons and provide their attributions and uses within their respective traditions. There is also a brief invocation to each god as well as a description of their magical images that enables one to make contact with their magical force.

The way to approach each god is through ritual and meditation. You should set up an altar to your Patron deity somewhere in your home. It does not have to be large or elaborate; it could be on the top of an occasional table, or even a shelf. Your should place a statue or image of the god or goddess on the altar. You can place offerings on the altar or light candles upon it, but it should not be used for any other magical operations.

At least once a week, or once a day, ideally, you should perform a ritual for your god or goddess. Light a candle and a stick of appropriate incense and place them on the altar. Imagine that you are standing in a temple to your deity. There are many illustrations of ancient temples in books and many now contain computer reconstructions that you can mine for ideas. Remember you don't have to be too historically accurate or elaborate. It is easier to access magical power using a simple temple because it is easier to visualize. The Egyptian gods have cool, dark temples with tall lotus columns, while the Celts favor open glades.

Once you have decided on the layout of your temple, it is best to stick to this image. These imaginary temples have an objective reality on the inner planes and, over time, will develop as places of power where you meet with your deity.

In your mind's eye, place before you a giant statue of your deity with a cubic altar in front of it. Visualize a brazier of incense and an eternal flame before the altar.

Now place your imaginary temple over your earth-plane room. There is a knack to this. The temple altar should be in the position of its earth-plane counterpart. It does not matter if your room is too small to hold the astral temple; just pretend the earth-plane walls are not there. When you become proficient at this, the imaginary temple will feel just as real as the earth-plane temple. The eternal flame replaces the candle before the altar, and the golden brazier full of sweet-smelling incense replaces the humble stick of incense.

You can say the invocations I give in this book, or better still, you can make up your own. Whatever you choose to say should be heartfelt.

After you have performed the invocation, see a bright light pour down from the heavens and touch the top of the statue to form a halo of divine brilliance. See the light descend and make the statue a living object. Now you may commune with your Patron deity.

After you have finished, thank the deity and allow the light to withdraw from the statue. See it ascend through the roof and toward the stars. Place the incense stick and the candle on the altar and leave them as an offering. Allow reality to reassert itself.

Communing with the gods is a personal thing; however, some care should be taken in dealing with the information they provide. Although the gods in themselves are pure beings, you are approaching them through your psychic senses, which are easily influenced by the ego. This means that sometimes the god will appear to say whatever your lower self wants it to say. During such moments, it is likely that communications will emphasize how important you are in the cosmic picture. It is from such corrupted communications that messianic cults are born.

Likewise, psychic communications can be open to influence from entities that, by cosmic standards, are unbalanced or subjectively evil, and can lead the aspirant away from the truth. Cabbalists were able to check the messages they received from astral beings by cross-referencing it to the Biblical law. If it didn't fit in, then they would doubt the contact's validity.

More common is the stray entity, which has no particular wish other than to attract your attention and be heard. These are the earthbound parts of the dead who often try to get in touch with the living. There has been a popularist-spiritualist tradition that the dead somehow hold the answers for the living and a belief that death somehow gives a person an enlightened perspective. Alas, this is untrue. All that the postmortem period leaves behind is the soulless husk of the personality of the dead. This slowly breaks up over time, but until it does so, it sometimes has some measure of sentience and experiences its world as would an ordinary person. This would be useful if the person had knowledge of a subject while he or she was alive; but if the person did not have the information when he or she was alive, then it is unlikely that the person can provide it when he or she is dead.

The problem of psychic intrusions within these workings have lead many occultists to abandon the practice altogether. This is a pity as there is tremendous potential for our development if we let the beings of the inner astral realms communicate with us. All that is needed is a degree of ritual purity and a good helping of common sense.

Firstly, you have to aspire to the highest spiritual principle that the deity represents and only look for its positive expression. When looking at its myths, try to understand how the deity's most bizarre acts have the most benign and divine motives.

For example, in one myth, Diana turned Actaeon into a deer for the crime of seeing her while she bathed in the woods. Actaeon was then torn apart by his own hounds.

On the surface, this seems an evil thing for the goddess to do. After all, it was hardly Actaeon's fault that he stumbled across the bathing goddess; however, there is much more to this myth. Diana was the goddess of Nature—the divine manifesting in nature.

Actaeon had seen that divine wisdom existed all around him and this realization burned him. He saw his own animal nature and knew how it limited him. Instead of remaining with the goddess to realize how she also manifested in him, he was filled with fear about where his realization would lead him. He tried to return to his old life, but once you have seen the divine behind all material creation, life can never be the same again. Actaeon was destroyed by his own animal nature, which forced him to conform to what others considered to be normal.

All advice received from your deity should be deeply meditated on and intellectually questioned. If the deity will not, or cannot, explain its teaching, it is safer to discount its input. More often, deities will not give out specific personal advice, but will instead explain things in terms of principles and concepts.

In some respects, the deities are extensions of your own unconscious and should not be allowed to make daily decisions for you. They should never be allowed to command or tell you want to do.

Most of the time, your Patron god can deal with all your petitions and talisman empowerment. Sometimes, though, it is better that another god does the job and your Patron will tell you to petition another divinity. If, for example, your Patron was Apollo and you wanted a talisman to put in your car to make sure it remained mechanically sound, you would likely be referred to Hephaestus, who is the Greek pantheon's mechanic.

Non-Pagan magicians would approach another god or goddess automatically if they felt their request was outside their Patron's sphere of influence; however, a Pagan should always ask their Patron before approaching another deity. The Patron god may not think it is a good idea to approach another god, or may feel that it can do the work itself.

Some gods do not mix well. The ancient myths are full of situations where gods warred with each other. Horus would be extremely unhappy about you working with his enemy Set. Although throughout ancient Egypt there are drawings where the two are seen together as friends, the common conception is that they are sworn enemies and magically that is how things play out.

Hades and Demeter are another combination that could prove difficult, as are Uranus and Saturn.[1]

Never mix your pantheons—if you are using an Egyptian Patron, don't approach Venus to sort out your love life; look instead to Isis or Hathor. Each pantheon inspires something different from those who are involved with it, and it does not pay to confuse them with anything else. The Celtic gods tend to inspire emotions, poetry, and power; the Greeks have music, dance, and debating; while the Egyptians activate the powers of the higher mind.

It is worthwhile to point out that a Pagan who develops a close relationship with hir or her deity will have much better results using these types of talismans than a non-Pagan magician who is only visiting the system part-time.

Do not mix the techniques given in this chapter with others in the book. They are designed as a simple, stand-alone system for Pagans and others who do not like the elaborate systems of the other forms of Western talismans.

Pagan Talismans

There are three different ways of making Pagan talismans. They are ritual gifting, charging an object, and making a petition.

Ritual Gifting

Most pre-Christian Western societies had a tradition of throwing swords, jewelery, tripods, and metal objects into rivers or lakes. These objects were often marked with the name of the worshipper and the god or goddess for whom the gift was intended. At other times, these objects where engraved with the hope that the gifter would become well again or have victory in combat. Sometimes they were placed in the river as a sign of thanks to the goddess or god for good health or victory.

Although some of these lakes and rivers were sacred to local deities, often the offerings were made at these sites to others. This was because in Celtic and Shamanic traditions lakes were considered doorways to the Otherworld. Shorelines were considered to be the most sacred because they were where this world met the next.

Offerings should be made with the personality of the god or goddess that you are worshipping in mind. Musical instruments would be dedicated to Apollo, shields to Lugh, and sistrums to Isis or Bast, for example.

While you may show your devotion to, say, Apollo by casting your favorite guitar into the Thames, this is unnecessary. After all, it is unlikely that Apollo would have any need for your favorite six-string when he can play the music of the spheres.

The concept of sacrifice is talismanic. By killing an animal or throwing a weapon into a bog, you are creating an event on the material plane so that power might flow all the way down the levels of creation to earth. By sacrificing something, you are allowing its transition to another level. In modern times, the biggest thing you can sacrifice is your time and effort.

Like giving a present, it really is the thought that counts. If you are rich, you could sacrifice a lot of money on a golden tripod to your Patron deity, but as far as the deity is concerned, you may as well have given it the divine equivalent of a pair of plaid socks. Your Patron would much rather see its followers stop what they are doing and make a tripod out of dowel, glue, and gold paint.

It does not matter if your gift does not look the greatest, or that you have no real artistic talent. It is the time and effort you put into making it that is the most important. Anyone who has done similar work knows that it requires real dedication, which is better than money to your Patron.

So, if you want to make a sacrifice, make something for your deity. If your Patron is Apollo, write a song dedicated to him. Write it down, place your petition underneath it, and lay it in the Sun for a week before burning it before his altar.

Many deities love flowers, but those grown in your own garden are a real sacrifice of your time. So is a pledge to place fresh flowers on the altar of your deity for a month.

You should include a note with your petition. If your sacrifice is a painting, your petition should be included on the back. If it is flowers, your petition should be written on paper and attached to the stems.

Your petition should be something like this:

I, (insert your own name) humbly request that (insert Patron deity's name) intervene on the material plane on my behalf. If it be her (his) will, may (s)he swiftly come to my aid so that (write a sentence of what you want).

After the sacrifice has been prepared, visualize yourself in the inner temple as before. Read an appropriate invocation either from the lists that are included later in this chapter, or read one of your own. See the statue come alive. See your gift as what it represents in its perfection. Then present the deity with your gift and read your petition.

Sometimes you might want to make a gift to your god out of devotion or love without attaching a petition.

After the ritual has been performed, the offering should be destroyed. This should be done by casting it into a river, burning it, burying it, or tearing it into small pieces and casting it into the wind. Seeing your work destroyed in this manner really will show you the meaning of sacrifice, but at least you will know that your gift is in the hands of your deity.

Charging an Object

When you want a talismanic object that you can carry around with you to radiate the power of a god or goddess, you charge a symbol or object that connects you to your deity. It could be an amulet of protection if you are traveling, or for job success if you were going for a job interview. The object could be anything from a stone to a necklace; however, it is usually best to select something that connects you to the god or goddess. A feather might be useful for Maat, or a drawing of a hammer for Thor.

Charging an object in a Pagan way involves bringing down the power of the god or goddess to the earthly levels. This requires knowledge of the deity's legends and a degree of preparation.

Set up an altar to the deity you wish to call to charge the object. It is important that you have an image of the deity before you and are as familiar with its form as you are the back of your hand. You should preferably have an image of the being close at hand to remind you what it looks like.

Relax as deeply as you can. Perform the Rite of Setting the Seals that is provided in the appendix of this book. This is a non-Cabbalistic version of the Banishing Ritual of the Pentagram and is designed for Pagans.

Light candles and incense to the deity and place the object that you wish to have empowered on the altar. Visualize yourself standing in the deity's imaginary temple. Make your invocation to the deity. See a light appear from the highest part of the sky and descend into the inner-plane temple, activating the statue so that it becomes a living, breathing entity. Make your request that the object be charged with the being's power for a particular purpose.

If the god agrees, shift your consciousness to the earth plane. Imagine that a small statue of the deity is at your feet. See it grow within you until it is about level with your eyes. Then enter into mind-to-mind contact with the deity. Allow the inner and outer temple to overlap, and see yourself as part-human and part-god, standing in it.

When you have achieved this, hold the object in your hands and say:

I who am the god(dess) (insert name) do bless and empower this physical object with my power. Henceforth it shall represent my power on earth and enable the bearer to (insert the object's purpose).

See a white light descend from the heavens through the head of the deity and down your spine to your heart. From there, the energy radiates down your arms into your hands and into the object. See the object absorb the power like a sponge. More power comes from the heavens until the physical object cannot take anymore and positively glows with energy.

Place the object on the altar and allow the god or goddess to shrink down to your feet. Step out of the godform and go to the other side of the altar. Shift your consciousness until it is entirely in the inner temple. Thank the deity for its blessing and see the light depart the temple.

Allow the images to melt away, and let the material world dominate your consciousness again.

Once the object has completed its work, it must be destroyed. Since such an object is created on the astral and the physical levels, and it must be destroyed on both.

The most effective way of doing this on the physical level is to throw the object into a deep, wide river or sea. Water is a good conductor of energy and helps to disperse the energy from the object. Another good method is to bury the object in at least three feet of earth. Earth slowly draws the energy out of the object. Burning the object is another option.

By removing the physical form of the object, you are removing the earth-plane focus of the energy and returning its focus to the inner planes; however, that is not the end of the object's life. As you destroy the object, you must contact the being that created it. Visualize yourself in the deity's temple. Invoke the deity and see the light activate its statue. Then, after thanking the deity for its help, imagine yourself holding a copy of the object and handing it to the deity. The deity will draw the object into its heart and then depart.

Petitioning the Gods

As we discussed in chapter 2, petitioning the gods is the most ancient way of making objects of power. Basically, this entails writing a letter to your deity and asking it to intervene on your behalf. It becomes an act of faith between you and your deity.

Katadesmoi, as described in chapter 2, were more often made by people who lacked magical training. During the same period of history, there were those who used them as the focus for more intensively magical rather than religious practices. These were designed to make sure that the prayer on the Katadesmoi worked, which seemed to bind the gods to obey the will of the magician.

Let me just say that there is no one alive who has the power to bind a god to do his or her will. Even those adepts who are not incarnate and who hold the keys to the magic of the universe could achieve such an act, even if their perfected natures allowed it.

I have read ancient texts where the magician appears to command the gods to obey him; however, if you look closely at these spell books, it is clear that the magician achieves this by identifying with the deity whom they are calling so strongly that he becomes an expression of its power. The magician aims for such a strong identification with his god or goddess that he can almost "command" other divine beings to make events happen. They do not see themselves as their deity but as a vessel for its force. This is similar to the object-charging exercise mentioned before.

To petition your deity, you should write the deity a letter on a single side of paper on the day of the week that corresponds to that being.[2] At the top, you should put a symbol of the deity—a thunderbolt for Jupiter, a spear for Horus, a quill pen for Thoth, and so on. Underneath this symbol, you should write:

> "In the name of the Most High god, I, (insert your name) petition the great god(dess) (insert goddess' name). O (insert goddess' name), manifest your power unto me so that (insert your intention here)."

Keep your intention brief and concise. Do not tell the gods exactly how you want things to happen—it is best to leave that to them. A bad example would be, "I would like to work in the computing department of McBison's Plastic Extrusions." Despite the fact that you might think you want to work at McBison's, your true aim is to find yourself a job in which you can be happy and successful. It is better to write, "I would like to find a job in which I could be happy and successful." Then, if your deity thinks that McBison's is the place for you, it will make it happen. It might be that McBison's would not make you happy in the long run and you would be better suited to a job in another company.

Next, get your deity's attention with a little ritual. Set up an altar to the deity and light appropriate an incense and a single candle.

Imagine yourself in the inner temple of the deity. Make your invocation to the statue and see the light appear from the highest part of the sky and descend into the statue, making it come alive. Light the incense and say:

As this offering smoke rises, may my petition and prayers to thee, O god(dess) (insert goddess' name), ascend to your sacred feet.

Then light the candle and say:

Great, mighty, and holy art thou, O light bearer, as this sacrifice is made, may you hear my prayer.

Now place your Katadesmoi on the altar and visualize your deity take it and read it. It may give you an indication that your request has been granted, but even if it does, you should ask for a sign on earth that your petition has been heard.

There will be signs associated with your deity. A surprise thunderstorm would be an appropriate one for Thor, or a surprise experience of a hawk if your deity were Horus. A book about the god or goddess may fall into your hands, or a friend may give you an item of jewelry associated with that deity.[3]

Thank the deity and see it depart. Take your petition, roll it up tightly, and tape it shut. Now it must be symbolically placed near something that can be clearly associated with the petition. If the petition is for money, put it in your wallet; if it is for love, place it close to your heart; if it is for protection from a particular person, try to get it as close to that person as possible (without the person seeing it); if it is to help you pass an exam, try putting it in your study notes and taking it into the exam with you.

When it is clear that the petition has been heard, you should perform a little thank-you ritual to your deity. This should involve you ascending to your inner temple, invoking the deity, and personally thanking the deity *even if it gave you a result you did not want.* In hindsight, you will be glad you received the result that you did.

The Gods

This section aims to give you a brief introduction to the incenses, colors, and planetary attributions (occultists call these *correspondences*) associated with eleven gods of Western mystery tradition Pagan pantheons. Obviously, you can do your own research and uncover your own associations, but these correspondences are the ones that have worked for me.

I have divided the gods into planetary groups, because it is easier for a talisman builder to see them by their functions, rather than by their theological meanings. In

Table 7
Pagan gods assigned to planets.

Planet	Greek	Roman	Egyptian	Norse	Celtic/Irish
Pluto	Hades	Pluto	Osirus	Odin	Pwyll
Uranus	Uranus	Janus	Set	Loki	Gwydion
Neptune	Poseidon	Neptune	Hapi	Njord	Manannan
Saturn	Kronos	Saturn	Isis	Frigg	Ceridwen
Jupiter	Zeus	Jupiter	Amon	Norns	Taranis
Mars	Ares	Mars	Horus	Thor	Morrigan
Venus	Aphrodite	Venus	Bast	Freya	Rhiannon
Mercury	Hermes	Mercury	Thoth	Bragi	Lugh
Sun	Apollon	Apollo	Ra	Frey	Bel
Moon	Artemis	Diana	Khons	Nanna	Epona
Earth	Demeter	Ceres	Geb	Ymir	Cerunnos

the Western mystery tradition, working with newly discovered planets like Pluto, Uranus, and Neptune is a modern phenomena. Rather than adding or changing planetary lists, many magicians in the Golden Dawn only work with the seven "old" planets—the Sun, the Moon, Mercury, Mars, Venus, Jupiter, and Saturn, as well as the lunar nodes.

Greek Gods

Hades

The god of the Underworld. He can provide help to find information involving past events and hidden secrets. His incense is holly or oregano. He is depicted as a dark king, usually in the colors of night and winter. His symbol is a helmet of darkness. His invocation is:

> *I call into the depths of the earth, to the kingdom of Hades. I request an audience with the king of the Underworld, Mighty Hades. Come forth unto this, thy temple.*

Uranus

The sky god who rules science, magic, inspiration, and change. He can provide help in all these matters, particularly if speed or sudden change is of the essence. His incenses are red storax and hyacinth. He is dressed in the colors of a starlit sky. His symbol is a phallus with testicles. His invocation is:

> *I call into the heavens to the starlit kingdom of Uranus. I request an audience with the first father of all. Come forth, King Uranus, unto this, thy temple.*

Poseidon

The god of the sea and earthquakes. He can assist with anything having to do with intuition, dreams, psychic powers, addictions, the entertainment industry, and mysteries. His incenses are camphor, elm, and willow. His color is sea green, and his symbol is a white horse or a trident. His invocation is:

> *I call into the deepest oceans to the sunken kingdom of Poseidon. I request an audience with the lord of the waves. Come forth, King Poseidon. Come forth, Earth shaker, unto this, thy temple.*

Kronos

The god who rules death and time. He can help with issues of inheritance, discipline, agriculture, past-life work, and aging. His incenses are cumin, myrrh, and black poppy. His color is black, and his symbol is a flint scythe or a crow. His invocation is:

> *I call into the fields of Greece where the second father of the Earth dwells and is harvested. Come forth, Kronos, king of time and death, unto this, thy temple.*

Zeus

The ruler of the gods. He can help with issues relating to the law, wealth, opportunity, morality, luck, education, and philosophy. His incenses are ash, sage, and basil, and his symbol is a thunderbolt. His invocation is:

> *I call unto the throne of Mount Olympus where the third father of the Earth dwells and is king. Come forth, Zeus, king of the gods, unto this, thy temple.*

Ares

The warrior of the gods. He can help with issues relating to physical desires, sex, conflict, surgery, courage, and manufacturing. His incenses are pepper, tobacco, and rowan oil, and his symbols are a sword and a ram. His invocation is:

I call unto Mount Olympus where the fires of the Earth are stoked. Come forth, Ares, warrior of the gods, unto this, thy temple.

Aphrodite

The goddess of love and beauty. She can help with issues relating to love, pregnancy, creativity, growth, music, art, and unions. Her incenses are rose, sandalwood, and musk. Her symbols are a dove and a girdle. Her invocation is:

I call unto Mount Olympus where the love of the gods dwells. Come forth, Aphrodite, divine love born of sea and foam, unto this, thy temple.

Apollon

The god of the Sun, healing, and music. He can help with health, authority, advancement, dancing, and musical ability. His incenses are frankincense, saffron, and orange. His symbols are a bow and arrow and a seven-string harp. His invocation is:

I call unto Mount Olympus where the heart of the Sun dwells. Come forth, Apollon, divine musician and healer, unto this, thy temple.

Hermes

The god of thieves and journalists, writing, speech, and travel. He can help with all matters of communication and magic. His incenses are lavender, cinnamon, and cloves. His symbols are winged sandals and a caduceus. His invocation is:

I call unto Mount Olympus where the messenger of the gods dwells. Come forth, thrice-greatest Hermes, unto this, thy temple.

Artemis

The virgin goddess of the Moon and hunting. She is helpful in dealing with instincts, moods, depression, and obsession. She can also help people understand their feminine natures. Her incenses are myrtle, camphor, and jasmine. Her symbols are a silver bow and arrows. Her invocation is:

> *I call unto mountains of Greece where the virgin goddess hunts. Come forth, Artemis, bearer of the silver lunar bow, unto this, thy temple.*

Demeter

The Mother Earth and corn goddess. She is helpful with healing and finding children, fertility, agriculture, dealing with death, money, and the home, material objects, and finding that which is lost. Her incenses are lilly, storax, and dittany of Crete. Her symbol is an ear of corn. Her invocation is:

> *I call unto the four quarters of the Earth where the great mother goddess roams searching for her daughter Persephone. Come forth, Demeter, mother of life on Earth, unto this, thy temple.*

Roman Gods

The Romans almost universally adopted the Greek gods—they just gave them different names. The images, colors, symbols, and invocations remain the same; all you need to do is substitute Jupiter for Zeus, Ceres for Demeter, and so on; however, this is not to say that they are the same deities.

There are subtle differences between the Roman and Greek gods that the different names help to key into. Generally, the Roman gods are more serious and solid than the Greek gods; they are more "moral" and reliable. Some consider the Roman gods to be too stodgy and a little withdrawn, however, they do have some good qualities. For example, Aphrodite's cruel streak is less obvious in Venus, and Jupiter is less despotic than Zeus.

Egyptian Gods

There is little information about appropriate incenses to use with specific Egyptian gods. The only recipe that has survived is for a temple incense called Kyphie. It can be obtained from many esoteric shops and is well worth finding. You may use frankincense and myrrh, which were also fairly common at the time. Alternatively, you can use the incenses recommended for the Greek and Roman gods.

Osirus

The god of resurrection and ruler of the dead. He is helpful when dealing with deep psychological trauma, phobias, religion, and obsessions, and can provide teaching on esoteric subjects. His color is green, and his symbol is either an ear of corn or a crook and flail. His invocation is:

> *I call to the lands of the west to the place where the Sun sets. Hail to thee, Osirus, lord of Amenti. I pray that you dwell among us in this, thy temple.*

Set

A star god of deserts and storms. He is helpful in removing blocks to development, providing spiritual power, realizing your darker side, and those things that you keep hidden; however, his energy is somewhat tainted. Although Set has been considered a "good" god at some points in his history (some pharaohs were even named after him), more often he was the "bad guy" of the Egyptian pantheon and was associated with Apep, Typhon, and Satan. This is particularly true if you accept the Osirian myth where he kills his brother and assumes the throne. His color is red, and his symbol is a wand. His invocation is:

> *I call beyond the east to the holy land of Khem. Hail to thee, Set, lord of the desert and the stars. I pray that you dwell among us in this, thy temple.*[4]

Hapi

The god of the Nile. He is helpful in providing material and spiritual wealth and nourishment, and protection during travel, particularly across water. His color is blue, and his symbol is a lotus crown. His invocation is:

> *I call beyond the east to the holy land of Khem. Hail to thee, Hapi, lifeblood of Khem, ruler of the water ways. I pray that you dwell among us in this, thy temple.*

Isis

The goddess of magic, motherhood, and death. She is helpful during childbirth, in dealing with death and change, in providing magical teachings, and with divination, healing, protection, and sexual dysfunction. Her color is blue, and her symbols are a throne and a vulture. Her invocation is:

> *I call beyond the east to the holy land of Khem. Hail to thee, Isis, mistress of magic, holder of the keys of life and death. I pray that you shall dwell among us in this, thy temple.*

Amon

The self-created ruler of the gods. He is helpful in the expansion of goals, creativity, generation, reproduction, and material and spiritual wealth. His color is gold, and his symbols are a ram and two plumes. His invocation is:

> *I call beyond the east to the holy land of Khem. Hail to thee, Amon, self-existent one, ruler of all the gods. I pray that you shall dwell among us in this, thy temple.*

Horus

The avenger god and slayer of evil. He is helpful in providing protection, courage, overcoming fears, setting wrongs right, overcoming phobias, and achieving victories. His colors are gold and yellow, and his symbols are a spear and a hawk. His invocation is:

> *I call beyond the east to the holy land of Khem. Hail to thee, Horus, son of Osirus. O thou who art the avenger of thy father, and the living Sun on Earth, I pray that you shall dwell among us in this, thy temple.*

Bast

The goddess of love, protection, and the home. She is helpful in providing protection (particularly in the home) from emotional upsets. She can also help with domestic harmony and courage, aid heart trouble, and enhance creativity. Her colors are black and blue, and her symbols are a cat and the lotus wand. Her invocation is:

I call beyond the east to the holy land of Khem. Hail to thee, Bast, lady of the east and power of love. I pray that you shall dwell among us in this, thy temple.

Thoth

The master of magic. He is helpful in anything to do with writing, mathematics, communication, and magic. His colors are green and yellow, and his symbols are an ibis bird and an ape. His invocation is:

I call beyond the east to the holy land of Khem. Hail to thee, Thoth, master of magic and words. I pray that you shall dwell among us in this, thy temple.

Ra

The Sun god. He is helpful with healing, growth (both material and spiritual), security, ruling your inner kingdom, and justice. His colors are gold and white, and his symbols are a hawk and a sun disk. His invocation is:

I call beyond the east to the holy land of Khem. Hail to thee, Ra, creative force who spreads out his wings. I pray that you shall dwell among us in this, thy temple.

Khonsu

The Moon god. He provides guidance, generative power, healing (particularly of the mind), and powers of exorcism. His color is silver, and his symbols are a crescent moon and sometimes a hawk. His invocation is:

I call beyond the east to the holy land of Khem. Hail to thee, Khonsu, navigator of the stars who crosses the skies in his boat. I pray that you shall dwell among us in this, thy temple.

Geb

The Earth god. He can provide material and spiritual wealth and help with agriculture, fertility, and creation. He helps the dead transform themselves by freeing them from the bonds of their bodies. His colors are black and green, and his symbols are the goose and the erect phallus. His invocation is:

I call beyond the east to the holy land of Khem. Hail to thee, Geb, who out of love created the gods. O sacred Earth, I pray that you shall dwell among us in this, thy temple.

Norse

There is limited information on Norse incense (or even if they used any). Fire seems to be important in their rituals and so incense could be replaced with candles; otherwise, use the standard planetary incenses. Ritual weaponry like swords, hammers, and knives also play a part in Norse rituals.

If you are lucky enough to have a medieval arsenal for your Norse workings, you can use weapons like wands to salute your deity. Pouring libations to the gods, your friends, your relatives, yourself, the government, people you may have met on the bus, and any small pets you might have is almost mandatory in this tradition.

Odin

The god of death, wisdom, and magic. He can provide teaching on magical matters and help solve mental and physical problems. He was the rune master and can help with divination. His symbols are the raven and the wolf. His invocation is:

I call beyond the Rainbow Bridge to the halls of Asgard. Hail to thee, Odin, walker between the worlds of life and death. O wise one, I pray that you shall dwell among us in this, thy hall.

Loki

The trickster, healer, and magician. He can provide solutions to all manner of problems in an unusual way. He teaches cunning and adaptation. His symbol is fire. His invocation is:

I call beyond the Rainbow Bridge to the halls of Asgard. Hail to thee, Loki, the wise and clever. O swift-tongued seer of truth, I pray that you shall dwell among us in this, thy hall.

Njord

The god of the sea, fishing, and prosperity. He can provide protection for journeys over water and into the subconscious mind. He is particularly useful in teaching meditation. His symbol is a long ship. His invocation is:

I call beyond the Rainbow Bridge to the halls of Asgard. Hail to thee, Njord, blameless ruler of men. I pray that you shall dwell among us in this, thy hall.

Frigg

The mother goddess and Odin's wife. She is associated with marriage, prophecy, and fate, and is a guide to the Underworld. Her symbols are cloud threads and a jeweled spinning wheel. Her invocation is:

I call beyond the Rainbow Bridge to the halls of Asgard. Hail to thee, Frigg, mother of goodness, beauty, and eloquence. Spinner of fate, I pray that you shall dwell among us in this, thy hall.

Norns

A triad of goddesses—Urd, Verdana, and Skuld—who weave the fate of the gods and humanity. Urd controlled the past, Verdana the present, and Skuld oversaw the future. They are useful in understanding the past, present, and future. Their symbols are a loom and spinning wheel. Their invocation is:

I call beyond the Rainbow Bridge to the halls of Asgard. Hail to the Norns, Urd, Verdana, and Skuld. Weavers and spinners of fate's fabric, I pray that you shall dwell among us in this, thy hall.

Thor

The god of storms and fertility, and defender of the world order. He controls the winds and teaches bravery, self-confidence, and friendship. His symbols are a hammer and the thunder. His invocation is:

I call beyond the Rainbow Bridge to the halls of Asgard. Hail Thor, lord of thunder, master of the winds of the Western world. Mighty warrior, I pray that you shall dwell among us in this, thy hall.

Freya

The goddess of love and poetry. She helps provide fertility, wealth, and prophecies, and is a guide to the Underworld. She teaches magic to women, helps both sexes in matters of the heart, and teaches creative writing. Her symbol is a falcon. Her invocation is:

> *I call beyond the Rainbow Bridge to the halls of Asgard. Hail Freya, the two-edged sword. Goddess of love and death, I pray that you shall dwell among us in this, thy hall.*

Bragi

The god of poetry, wisdom, and words. He is the god of writers, journalists, and librarians. He also speaks the truth and is unafraid to do so. He can provide confidence in self-expression and teaches his wisdom to others. His symbols are an apple of eternal youth and a pen. His invocation is:

> *I call beyond the Rainbow Bridge to the halls of Asgard. Hail Bragi, best son of Odin, truth speaker. Mighty forger of words, I pray that you shall dwell among us in this, thy hall.*

Frey

The god of fertility. He is helpful in making changes to the weather and providing peace, plenty, and prosperity. His symbols are a horse and an erect phallus. His invocation is:

> *I call beyond the Rainbow Bridge to the halls of Asgard. Hail Frey, god of the world, and rider of the solar chariot. Bringer of bounty, I pray that you shall dwell among us in this, thy hall.*

Nanna

The Moon goddess. She is helpful in developing deep relationships that pass beyond death. She deals with subconscious afflictions. Her symbol is the Moon itself. Her invocation is:

I call beyond the Rainbow Bridge to the halls of Asgard. Hail Nanna, wife of beauty. Revealer of true love, I pray that you shall dwell among us in this, thy hall.

Ymir

The giant whose body makes up the Earth. He is helpful in anything to do with the physical earth, sky, sea, trees, mountains, and housing. He is in charge of hail and snow. His symbol is all you see around you. His invocation is:

I call beyond the sight of mortals, who see but do not. Hail Ymir, body of the world. I pray that we shall see you as you dwell among us in this, thy hall.

Celtic/Irish

Since the ancient Celts left nothing in the way of writings, we are left with oral myths and legends that were not put in print until the Middle Ages. We also have some of the hearsay commentary written by the Greeks and Romans who were enemies of the Celts. These sources give the impression that there was a universal system among the Celts rather than a very diverse collection of regional gods and goddess. These were associated with springs, lakes, rivers, and mountains. Early Celts had no concept of gods and goddesses that were in human form. The Celtic leader Brennus, who was defeated at the battle of Delphi in 279 B.C., laughed when he was told that the Greeks believed in gods that had human forms.

Generally, the Celts believed in a triune god similar to the Christian concept of the Trinity. In addition to this, there were batteries of important goddesses.

Most Neo-Pagans, however, adopt the Celtic tradition as seen through the eyes of the Middle Age legends—particularly the Mabinogion for the Welsh-Celtic tradition and the Irish *Book of Leinster* for the Irish Celts.

In mixing the two traditions, I have selected deities who are closest to the planetary natures needed for talisman work.

Once again, we have no recorded incense for the Celts, so I suggest using the planetary ones that have been listed for the Greeks.

Pwyll

The lord of the Underworld. He can help you adapt to your current situation, exorcise evil, learn secrets of friendship, see visions, and understand love. His symbols are a badger and a hunting horn. His invocation is:

> *I call to the ancient land of Dyved. Come forth, Pwyll, King of Annwvyn, and slayer of the unslayable, visionary on the sacred mound of Arberth. Be welcome in this, thy hall.*

Gwydion

The god of magic. He can help answer riddles, make changes in your life, heal, and teach magic and music. He can find the light in the darkness of any situation. His symbols are the ash tree, a stag, a sow, and a wolf. His invocation is:

> *I call to the ancient land of Gwynedd. Come forth, Gwydion, master of magic and music, bringer of light to all. Be welcome in this, thy hall.*

Ceridwen

The goddess of wisdom and death. She has the ability to bring about change, to provide wisdom, and to show people the essence of their lives through many incarnations. Her symbol is the Caldron of Wisdom, and her symbol is a sow. Her invocation is:

> *I call into the mists of time to the land between this and the next. Come forth, Ceridwen, dark mother and guardian of the grail. Be welcome in this, thy hall.*

Manannan

The sea god. He can act as a guide to the Otherworld and the land of the dead. He is also a protector during journeys by sea, He can teach us how to master our emotions and can help devise cunning plans for our lives. His symbol is his boat, Ocean Sweeper; his horse, Aonbarr; and his sword, the Answerer. His invocation is:

> *I send my voice to the Isle of Man. Come forth, Manannon, lord of the sea, guide to the Land of Youth and rider of the Waves. Be welcome in this, thy hall.*

Taranis

The thunder god. He was strongly identified by the Romans and Gauls with Jupiter, and, as a ruler and bringer of luck, he is similar to Jupiter. His symbols are the lightning flash and the wheel (possibly similar to the idea of the Wheel of Fortune in a Tarot deck). His invocation is:

> *I call to the ancient land of Gaul where Taranis has his throne. Hail to thee, thunderer and light bringer. Be present in this, thy hall.*

Morrigan

The war goddess. She can help you face death, predict the future, and provide bravery in the midst of impossible odds. She can also help in developing skills in magic—although she tends to teach through experience. Her symbols are a raven, a spear, a cow, and a wolf. Her invocation is:

> *I approach the Washer of the Ford, between this world and next. Hail to thee, specter queen, Morrigan. I ask you to attend this, thy hall, and bring thy blessings.*

Rhiannon

The horse goddess. She can provide protection and speed during journeys on the astral or physical planes. She can act as a guide to the Otherworld. She can teach motherhood, creativity, and loyalty. Her symbol is a horse. Her invocation is:

> *I call to the ancient land of Dyved. Hail to thee, great Queen Rhiannon, ruler of this world and next. Come forth into this, thy hall, and bring thy blessings.*

Lugh

The light god. He can help us understand and learn all arts and skills, including war and healing. The Romans believed that he was Mercury, and he does have similar attributions. His symbols are a rod sling, magical spear, and a dog. His invocation is:

> *I call into the Otherworld. Hail to thee, Shining One. Hail to thee, Inventor of all Arts. Welcome, Lugh, to this, thy hall.*

Bel

The solar light and fire god. He is very closely linked to Apollo and adopted many similar attributions. He can help provide fertility and growth, both material and spiritual. His symbols are two fires, which are sometimes seen as a gateway between this world and the next. His invocation is:

I call between the two flaming columns and call the light into this sacred place. Hail to thee, Bel, midsummer's flame, be welcome in this, thy hall.

Epona

The lunar goddess of pathways. She can help with journeys of all kinds. She provides maternal strength and love. She can open pathways through strife and conflict. Her symbols are a white horse and mare's milk. Her invocation is:

I call along the Ridgeway of Albion at the place of the white horse. Come forth, Epona of the sacred way. Be present in this, thy place.

Cernnunos

The horned Earth god. He can help in matters of nature, virility, fertility, and rebirth. His symbols are deer antlers, a snake, and a torque. His invocation is:

I call thee, Horned One, god of this World and Next. Hail to thee, lord of the animals. Hail to thee, life of all. Be welcome in this, thy hall.

---

1. Hades stole Demeter's daughter, Persephone, and carried her off to the Underworld. Demeter mourned and threw the world into a perpetual winter. Saturn castrated his father, Uranus.
2. Monday, the Moon; Tuesday, Mars; Wednesday, Mercury; Thursday, Jupiter; Friday, Venus; Saturday, Saturn; and Sunday, the Sun.
3. This is a simpler version of the "checks on earth" formula (signs following) that we will be looking at in chapter 10.
4. Set is mentioned for completeness; however, it is my experience that magicians who call upon Set (Crowley being a case in point) have historically tended to be affected negatively. If you agree, you could use Isis for Uranus; if you disagree, at least I have warned you.

5

Angels and Talismans

Angels play an important role in the manufacture of Cabbalistic talismans. They act as transformers of divine power, drawing it through the levels of creation and harnessing it in a manner in which it can be used practically.

The word *angel* comes from the Greek word *Angelos*, which means "messenger"; however, they are not the winged creatures of the Victorian pre-Raphaelites. They do not spend their lives playing harps or running between the throne of God and humanity, with notes from the Almighty. If Divinity is white light, angels are the spectrum in which it is divided. Angels are the One God as it interacts with its creation.

As the One manifests through the four levels of creation (see chapter 1), it becomes denser as it begins to form individual objects. By the time the Unity reaches the material plane, these objects are so dense that the divine conscious has slowed almost to a stop.

If scientists had multidimensional cutting tools and sliced into an object to see its spiritual layers, they would identify four different "grades" of Divinity. Further testing would reveal that each of these levels had a consciousness. If you were sufficiently psychic, you could contact these different types of consciousness and could name them. Rather than being names of Unity, they would be the names of divine fragments—the names of angels. They would be so specialized that they would appear to have an individuality or personality.

Some people may disagree with my definition of angels and point to Biblical verses where angels appear to deny their divinity and refuse to let themselves be worshipped as God. Such verses, though, are not inconsistent with my definition.

The Jews were strict monotheists who wanted to worship One God instead of a pantheon of different gods with different functions in nature. If they moved to worshipping different functions of God, they would be no different from other "Pagan" religions of the time. Angels would simply replace the old gods, and the spiritual subtleties that they found in true monotheism would be lost.

Since angels are involved in the administration of the universe, throughout history humanity has tended to see them organized into a hierarchical structure mirroring our own. This is not because angels actually work this way, but because we humans have a tendency to think that our methods of organization are the best. So they tended to see God as a king, surrounded by chancellors who each commanded "lesser men" whose functions were gradually more specialized.

In esoteric terms, this hierarchy was, in descending order: god, archangels, angels, intelligences, and spirits. Archangels were usually the head of an order, or choir. The goal of this choir was usually fairly general, but the angels who were members had specific tasks.

Camael, for example, was the head of the protective angels,[1] who are sometimes called Powers or Kerebim.[2] The Kerebim's task is to administer divine justice on all levels, so the choir is composed of angels of punishment and of fear, and of angels charged with the control of demons, and so on. These angels control lesser angels who work closer to the physical level, managing things like police forces, courts, lawyers, and jails in the human world.

Some people may consider that in a world full of miscarriages of justice, embezzling lawyers, and corrupt police there might be something wrong with the work practices of the Powers; but it should be considered that the Powers administer cosmic justice based on the workings of the universe rather than our criminal justice system or even our perceptions of "right" and "wrong." The workings of divine justice have been a mystery to many religions as they see the good suffer and the bad prosper. Their general conclusion is that it all balances out in the end.

If we return to our four-level diagram of creation in chapter 1, we can see that the archangels exist in the second world, or the realm of Briah. Angelic choirs rule the level of Yetzirah.

There is a third level of beings who work on the lower astral plane where the physical world (Assiah) and the astral plane (Yetzirah) meet. These are called *spirits*, and their exact definition is controversial. Some people consider them to be angelic because they represent the divine energy at its lowest level—the spark behind all matter. In traditional occultism, these spirits are often called *elementals*. They are divided into four classes in accordance with their natures—earth, water, air, and fire. Angels actually manipulate combinations of elementals when they wish to bring something about on the physical plane.

Because elementals are neutral forces, which are neither good nor evil, some people are reluctant to class them as angels; however, an order of angels called the *Ashim* ensoul each elemental, networking them into the great hierarchy of angels.

Planetary energies have their own spirits. These spirits are similar to the elementals in that they operate in the same lower astral world; they are blind forces, which can be used for good or evil; and angels control them. While the Ashim ensoul the elementals, an angel of a planet ensouls the planetary forces.[3] For example, Hanael ensouls the spirit of Venus—Anael—and Cassiel ensouls the spirit of Jupiter—Hismael.

Much like humans, who do not see the activity of their souls, the angelic ensoulment of a planet's spirit is passive. The daily running of the planetary force is carried out by a personality or intelligence.

Occultists use these intelligences when they want to gain direct control of a planetary force without getting their fingers burnt. Using a computer analogy, the spirit is the energy whizzing about the silicon chip, the intelligence is the program language that controls the energy, and the planetary angel is the program.

Planetary spirits have a direct influence over elementals and are capable of making new things happen on Earth, which is why they are so important in magic or talisman making.

As I mentioned earlier, since angelic society mirrored their own hierarchies, magicians believed that they could gain control over the lesser angels and elementals by doing what they did in their own society. There were two methods of doing this—the direct personal approach, which required knowing who to speak to, or patronage by a higher authority.

In Europe, until the nineteenth century, government was based on patronage. You could get what you wanted by having a powerful friend who approached the appropriate department on your behalf.

Madeline Montalban's angelic system (which we discussed in chapter 2) involved a simple patronage system that used mostly the angel of the Moon, Gabriel, to contact the others.

She also hinted at another useful patronage system, which involved approaching your solar and lunar angels. These were archangels that Montalban believed were linked to you at birth and had the strongest affinity with your personality. Their allocation was based on your astrological Sun and Moon signs. If your Sun was in Leo, your solar angel was Michael; if it was in Scorpio, your solar angel was Samael.

Table 8
Angels and their attributions to signs of the zodiac.

Sign of the zodiac	Angel
Aries	Samael
Taurus	Haniel
Gemini	Raphael
Cancer	Gabriel
Leo	Michael
Virgo	Raphael
Libra	Haniel
Scorpio	Samael
Sagittarius	Sachiel
Capricorn	Cassiel
Aquarius	Uriel
Pisces	Sachiel

Solar and lunar angels act as spirit guides, and, once contacted is established with them, they are used to introduce you to the various angels you intend to put on a talisman before consecration.

Once contact is made with the various beings, it is possible to ask them, via your Patrons, to work through the talisman you intend to create. If they agree to empower your talisman beforehand, it is unnecessary to proceed with long invocations asking them to perform their tasks.

"Meetings" between your Sun and Moon angels should take place in the Temple of Earth described later in this chapter. Then the three of you should pathwork to the appropriate astral temple to meet the archangel, angel, or planetary spirit you intend to approach for cooperation.

Another method for approaching a bureaucracy is to look at the "staff lists" of the angels and their many functions. Most magical books are so packed full of these that they look like astral telephone directories. The problem, however, is that these lists contradict one another. For example, some tell you that the angel of the Sun is Michael, while others insist that it is Raphael. Other lists give different planetary attributions to the angelic choirs and dispute their position on the Tree of Life.

Attempts have been made to codify all the angels; the Esoteric Order of the Golden Dawn made the last notable attempt. The truth is, though, that there is no one system that is totally correct—all of them work. For a while, I thought that there must be an angel of reconciliation who worked like an operator, connecting the call to the right department. This is possible, but I think it is more likely that we do this ourselves.

Inside all of us is the ability to connect to the angels. Like the angels, we have a part of ourselves that is a fragment of God. Our only difference is that, unlike angels, we were created to understand and move about creation. An angel completely understands its field, but cannot comprehend anything outside it. Try telling an angel of plant growth about hate, and you might as well be explaining what a computer is to a caveman; however, ask the angel about its speciality subject, and there is nothing the angel cannot tell you.

The exceptions to this rule are the archangels. All of creation is divided between them, so they tend to know everything, but they tend to see things on a scale that is too big for the average human to understand. They are like the board of directors of a car company; they may know everything their company does, but if you ask them how to change the spark plug in their latest model, they might refer you to one of their mechanics.

Humanity's divine spark enables the whole universe on all levels to be looked at and considered. It is part of human nature to explore and overcome challenges. We are built to move around the earth plane and even ascend to the throne of Deity itself. One of our first challenges is to find out who we are and realize that divine spark that enables us to communicate with the angels.

In the next chapter we will look at sigils. These are the signatures of the angels and are like "stamps" of their authority. Sigils were made in several ways—some were simply traditional patterns that do not seem to have any logical shape and the others were formed using magic squares.

The lists of angels I present here are (with some slight modifications) identical to those of the Esoteric Order of the Golden Dawn. Although other lists exist, I have found these to be the most useful and complete. You might find another list and prefer that one, but whatever you do, stick to it! Don't one day evoke Michael as the angel of the Sun and then decide the next day that he really belongs to Mercury.

Magic is based on subconscious programming. If for several years you associate Michael with the Cabbalistic sphere Tiphareth, then every time you think of Michael you will connect him with the Sun, healing, beauty, and everything else associated with that sphere. If suddenly you change your mind and associate Michael with Mercury, the energy you will unconsciously call into your Mercury talisman will be colored by solar and Tiphareth force.

Now let us look at the names of the archangels, angels, choirs, spirits, and intelligences that we will be using to make our talismans.

Archangels

The Cabbalists name eight archangels, one for each sphere on the Tree of Life. They also name two special archangels to mediate divine powers to Earth and the highest heaven. These were Sandalphon and Metatron (who, according to tradition, were originally human). Archangels work on the level of Briah.

Table 9

Archangels and their relationships to the planets and the Tree of Life.

Archangel	Sphere on the Tree of Life	Planetary association
Metatron מטטרון	Kether The Crown	None
Raziel רזיאל	Chockmah Wisdom	None
Tzaphqiel צפקיאל	Binah Understanding	Saturn
Tzadqiel צדקיאל	Chesed Wisdom	Jupiter
Khamael כמאל	Geburah Justice	Mars
Raphael רפאל	Tiphareth Beauty	Sun
Haniel האניאל	Netzach Victory	Venus
Michael מיכאל	Hod Glory	Mercury
Gabriel גבריאל	Yesod Foundation	Moon
Sandalphon סנדלפון	Malkuth Kingdom	Earth

Orders of Angels (Choirs)

Orders of angels are collections of angels functioning at the level of Yetzirah. An archangel (who is stationed at Briah) rules each order. This list comes from Moses Maimonides (in Mishne Torah), and it is similar to that of the Esoteric Golden Dawn. Both Maimonides and the Golden Dawn place the Yesod and the Seraphim in Geburah. I, however, have a problem placing the Seraphim in Geburah, as their function is to stand before the throne of God and chant, "Holy, Holy, Holy." This function is more related to Kether. However, the Kerubim which represent the highest form of the elements (fire, water, air, and earth) have a Kether-like function. In the Talmud, they are equated with the Order of Wheels, which are related to Chockmah. The Kerubim also have a protective nature and are depicted as temple and church guardians, which is a function related to Geburah.

Table 10
The orders of angels.

Order	Sphere on the Tree of life	Order Leader (Archangel)
Chayoth ha Qadesh (or Seraphim)	Kether	Metatron מטטרון
Auphanium	Chockmah	Raziel רזיאל
Arelim	Binah	Tzaphqiel צפקיאל
Chashmalim	Chesed	Tzadqiel צדקיאל
Kerubim[4]	Geburah	Khamael כמאל
Melekim	Tiphareth	Raphael רפאל

Order	Sphere on the Tree of life	Order Leader (Archangel)
Elohim[5]	Netzach	Haniel האניאל
Beni Elohim	Hod	Michael מיכאל
Tarhishim[6]	Yesod	Gabriel גבריאל
Ashim	Malkuth	Sandalphon סנדלפון

Archangels of the Planets

Angels are useful in making talismans. They are the members of the above orders (or choirs) and answer to the archangels, who are in charge of the Sepheroth. I have given the Hebrew name of the planets they are in charge of because some magicians prefer to use these on talismans instead of the English names.

You will notice from this list that most of the names are archangels of Sepheroth, so it may seem confusing to call them archangels of planets, too. To use a business analogy, these are like company directors who also have a job within the organization; however, it is important to note that there are some differences.

The archangels of the Sepheroth are universal—that is, their powers are expressed throughout all levels of creation throughout every galaxy in the universe. The archangels of the planets only have power within our solar system; however, because the solar system is part of the universe, planetary archangels are a subset of Sepherothic archangels.

Michael the archangel of the Sun is different from Michael the archangel of Tiphareth. This is because Michael, as archangel of the Sun, is only revealing a small part of his personality. It is as if he has had to leave part of himself behind in Briah in order to lower himself down to the Yetzaratic level to be the Sun archangel.

There are angels that can be used for more specific purposes. For example, Dumah is identified as the angel of dreams and can be used in talismans to help you

Table 11
Planets and angels.

Planet	Hebrew Name of Planet	Archangel Ruling the Planet
Saturn	Shabbathai שבתאי	Kassiel כסיאל
Jupiter	Tzedek צדק	Sachiel סחיאל
Mars	Madim מדם	Zamael זמאל
Sun	Shemesh שמש	Michael מיכאל
Venus	Nogah נוגה	Anael אנאל
Mercury	Kobab כובב	Raphael רפאל
Moon	Levanah לבנה	Gabriel גבריאל

understand your dreams. Alas, a list of all the angels is far beyond the scope of this book. Gustav Davidson's *Dictionary of Angels* contains long lists of all the angels and their job descriptions.

Angelic Planetary Intelligences

Angelic planetary intelligences are the brains of the planetary force. As such, they are easier to talk to on the astral plane than planetary spirits. They are complex creatures and show the good and bad characteristics of the planets they rule. For example, Graphiel, who is the intelligence of Mars, can be protective, but can also opt for a violent approach. Agiel, the intelligence of Saturn, can be good at sorting out inheritance problems, but tends to be slow to act.

When working with intelligences, it is vital to get the cooperation of and work through the appropriate archangel of the planet.

It is significant that the name of the intelligence of the Moon, Malkah be Tarshisim ve-ad Ruachoth Schechali, is longer than the others. This is because the lunar force is much more complicated than the forces of the other planets.

The ancients described twenty-eight types (or mansions) of the Moon, each having different meanings. Each mansion had its own intelligence, and in charge of all these was the intelligence of intelligences—Malkah be Tarshisim ve-ad Ruachoth Schechali. Although I have known people who have had some success working with specific mansion intelligences, I find that it is easier and just as effective to simply work with the intelligence of intelligences when making lunar talismans.

Table 12
Angelic intelligences.

Planet	Angelic Intelligence
Saturn	Agiel אגיאל
Jupiter	Iophiel יהפיאל
Mars	Graphiel גדאפיאל
Sun	Nakhiel נכיאל
Venus	Hagiel הגיאל

Planet	Angelic Intelligence
Mercury	Tiriel טיריאל
Moon	Malkah be Tarshisim ve-ad Ruachoth Schechalim מלכאבתרשישׂוער רוחותחלים

Spirits

There are magicians who like to get very close to the target of their magical operations. After magically badgering the divine name, the archangel of the sphere on the Tree of Life, the planetary archangel, and the intelligence, they are not happy unless they also control the planetary spirit.

Working with spirits, though, is a lot harder to do—a magician faces all the problems of dealing with a planetary intelligence, but without the brains. Spirits are a blind force and are almost impossible to reason with without the blessing of the intelligence or the angel of the planet.

Spirits operate closest to the physical realm, and any talisman tuned to their powers works more quickly and efficiently; but spirits are not that much further down in level from the more rational and easier-to-control intelligences, who they obey without question. If the intelligence agrees to ensoul a talisman, there is no doubt that the correct contrite spirit will be given the task and will do it properly.

The name for the spirit of the Moon is the spirit of spirits, rather that the twenty-eight separate spirits of each mansion.

Table 13
Planetary spirits.

Planet	Spirit
Saturn	Zazel זאזל
Jupiter	Hismael הסמאל

Planet	Spirit
Mars	Bartzabel
	ברצבאל
Sun	Sorath
	סורת
Venus	Qedemel
	קדמאל
Mercury	Taphthartharath
	תפתרתרת
Moon	Schad Barschemoth ha Shartathan
	שר ברשמעת השרתתן

Getting in Touch with Angels

Despite what some people believe, putting the names of angels with whom you have had no previous experience on a talisman is unlikely to be successful. Carefully placing an angel's name on a talisman that you have copied from an occult book will no more empower that talisman than copying "The child is in the airport" from a phrase book in a foreign language.

Traditionally, it was believed that angels would not come to those whom they did not know; however, this is not entirely true. There have been many occasions where angels have spontaneously appeared to people when called.

The reason for this anomaly is the fact that angels are both subjective and objective realities. On one hand, they are the rulers of distant stars, and yet on the other hand, they are part of you. Occultists call this *microcosmic* (the part of angel that is inside you and is subjective) and *macrocosmic* (the part of the angel that is connected to the stars and is objective).

One of the mainstays of occultism is the Hermetic maxim "As above, so below." In other words, what happens within you has a corresponding influence on what happens in the universe. When we relate this principle to angels, we can say that if you are in touch with the part of you that corresponds to that angel, then you are more likely to be able to contact the part of that angel that is macrocosmic.

That is all very well, but how do you contact the angelic part of yourself? This is a process of realization that transforms your life and is not something that can be done by reading a book. Such work, when performed correctly, actually lights up part of the aura. A psychic person can see the microcosmic angel as a little star that orbits the aura. When this level of angelic interaction is achieved, the diving permeates into the personality, leading to a definite change.

It takes time to achieve this ideal state, and angels are part of an involved magical spiritual tradition. Describing this tradition would fill another book, although some of its techniques are listed below.

It is unlikely that a magician, who will need to know the names of a legion of angels to prepare several simple talismans, will have the time to know that many angels intimately; however, it is my contention that everyone should take steps to approach all the archangels, angels, and intelligences before putting them on talismans, amulets, and charms. This means that talisman making will become part of many magicians' spiritual paths, and their construction will draw the magicians closer to that aspect of Deity.

The way to approach angels is to meet them halfway. The old ceremonial magical technique was fixated on the earth. It was believed that meeting an angel halfway meant building the angel a physical site that corresponded directly to the environment to which the angel belonged.

You would build a temple out of appropriate material, paint it in the right colors, furnish it with items connected to the angel, and eat only foods associated with the angel. Obviously, this is a little expensive and is hard work.[7] You could spend a fortune building a gold room in order to have a chat with the angel Michael, for example.

The modern approach is to meet the angels on the next level up—in the realms of your imagination, using a technique called *pathworking*.[8] In your imagination, the temple can be made of the finest materials, colored correctly, and filled with the most expensive props. Nearly impossible planetary configurations that are suitable for the meeting of the angels, or the consecration of their talismans, can fill the sky.

This begs the question that if imagination techniques, or pathworking, are so effective, then why didn't the ancients use them? The short answer is that they did. We have ancient texts that used pathworking as an aid to memory. There is an occult tradition, yet to be "proven," that early training in the Egyptian temples included similar techniques. It is commonly believed that it was only during the early ascendancy of Christianity that pathworking techniques declined.

Since the nineteenth century, occult Renaissance pathworking techniques have been rediscovered and used by modern magicians. There was a belief, borrowed from the Cabbalists, that there is an astral temple for each sphere on the Tree of Life, and each of these encapsulates every aspect of planetary and zodiacal energy. These astral temples contain all the relevant symbols associated with the planet and are an ideal place to meet planetary angelic contacts.

Astral Temples

There are ten main astral temples for Cabbalistic magic. Each has a different color, shape, and energy. There are different ways of getting to each astral temple, each leading to a different aspect of the sphere on the Tree of Life. The method I am going to describe to you is designed to contact the planetary aspect of the astral temple, which is one of the most important for the manufacture of talismans. If you do not have a connection with the planetary powers, your talisman will not have any energy.

Firstly, you will need to make a flashing tablet for the planet of the angel you are hoping to meet. Details of how to make these are given in chapter 7.

Before the pathworking, you should thoroughly relax and perform the Cabbalistic Cross and the Middle Pillar exercises described in chapter 3.

Once this vital work has been done, stare at your flashing tablet for a few minutes. Your aura will start to vibrate to the planetary energy that you are hoping to attract.[9]

Next, forming the intention of visiting the planetary temple and still looking at the flashing tablet, start to vibrate the divine name associated with the planet. For example, if you wished to visit the planet associated with Jupiter, you would choose the divine name El. Vibrate the divine name at least ten times.

Next, vibrate the name of the archangel of the sphere on the Tree of Life at least ten times. Using our Jupiter example, this would be Sachiel. Now close your eyes and, in your imagination, visualize the door of the temple appearing before you.

The sections that follow are pathworkings into the various planetary/Sepherothic temples. You might want to memorize these, record them on tape, or have a sympathetic friend read them for you.

Once you have finished the pathworking, thank the angels and then depart through the door from which you came. You should perform the Middle Pillar, Cabbalistic Cross, and Banishing Ritual of the Pentagram exercises before leaving the room, which will balance out any planetary influences that you may have attracted during the pathworking.

If you still feel unbalanced after performing these exercises, I recommend a further visualization of the earth temple. Don't call any more angels; just relax there for a few moments and the temple will help ground you. Then perform the Middle Pillar, Cabbalistic Cross, and Lesser Banishing Ritual of the Pentagram exercises again.

Earth Temple

Before you is a wooden door. Knock on it ten times and it will swing open into a temple. You are standing in the west, facing east. The wall in front of you is a greenish-lime color; the wall on the right is red brown, and the wall on your left is olive.

Lighting the cavern are ten huge green candles that are hooded so that their light reflects backward onto the walls. The floor is tiled with black-and-white alternating squares. In the center of the cavern is a black cubic altar with a single candle in a lead bowl and an equal-armed cross.

In the south, there is a bubbling pool of molten rock; in the north, a tall stone; in the west is a clear pool of water; and in the east, you can feel a draft of cool air.

Also in the east is a door, which is flanked by a black pillar on the left and a white pillar on the right. After you have performed your invocations, the archangels, angels, or spirits will appear from the door between these pillars.

Moon Temple

The door before you is silver with a crescent Moon stamped in it. Knock on the door nine times and it will swing open to reveal a silver temple with a pearl encrusted floor.

The temple is round and the roof is the violet of the night's sky. On the roof's borders are twenty-eight depictions of the Moon in all her mansions. There is a scent of myrrh in the air. Before you is a pair of silver sandals that you put on. Nine silver lanterns hang from the ceiling; their white candles make the pale white walls glow.

In the center of the temple is a pool of seawater that moves as if propelled by a hidden power. Floating in the pool's center, on an island, is an altar formed of pearl and silver. You can walk to the altar by stepping on the water, which miraculously holds your weight.

A single silver cross and a dish of water are on the altar.

East of the temple there is a door that is flanked by a silver-and-black pillar. Your contacts will come through this door.

Before the door is a statue of a woman riding a bull. Under the bull's feet is a crab. The statue is clothed in white, and on her head she wears a lunar crescent that is held by a crown made from two entwined serpents. In her right hand is an arrow, and in her left hand is a mirror. Entwined serpents are about her arms and feet.

Mercury Temple

Before you is a door that appears to be silver, but is mixed with all the colors of the rainbow. You knock on the door eight times and it swings open.

The floor is made of millions of multicolored gemstones that seem to shimmer and move in the light. The ceiling and walls are bright orange. Eight brass lanterns light the room. The ceiling is bordered with the countless names of Deity in a million languages.

In the southeast of the temple, there is a door flanked by a silver-and-black pillar. Your contacts will come through this door.

In the center of the room is a great pool of mercury, which, like the water of Yesod, you may cross to get to an altar of marble that reflects a rainbow light. There is a winged caduceus, a pine cone, and a single white candle on the altar.

In the east of the temple is a statue of a young, bearded man. In his left hand there is a caduceus, and in his right hand, a flute.[10] His feet are winged.

Venus Temple

Before you is a door of brass stamped with the symbol for Venus. You knock on the door seven times and it swings open to reveal a temple of emerald green.

Seven brass pillars uphold a roof that seems to have been carved from a single emerald. Hanging from the roof are seven lamps, each of a different color.

The walls are green and are covered with pictures of a cupid holding arrows of love.

At the temple's heart is an altar of brass on which has been placed a single rose and a lamp holding a single, still flame.

In the northeast of the temple, there is a door flanked by a silver-and-black pillar. Your contacts will come through this door.

In the east is a statue of a beautiful woman made of blue lapis lazuli. Crowned with seven stars, her long hair tumbles loosely down her back. She is wearing a long robe tied with a girdle and holds a laurel and an apple in her right hand. In her left hand she carries a comb.

Mars Temple

Before you is a door of iron with the symbol for Mars stamped on it. Knock on the door five times and it will swing open to reveal a temple shaped like a pentagon.

The floor is cast of red iron, and iron pillars uphold the scarlet ceiling. In the ceiling's center is a Tudor rose of five petals, and five iron lamps hang from the ceiling.

At the room's center is a huge altar cut from a single diamond that has a tall burning flame, which reaches almost to the ceiling. Surrounding the flame are the weapons of Justice—the sword and the spear. The spear lies in the east, the sword in the south, the helmet in the west, and the shield in the north.

In the southwest of the temple, there is a door flanked by a silver-and-black pillar. Your contacts will come through this door.

East of the altar is a diamond statue of a crowned man in armor riding on a lion. In his right hand is a naked sword, and in his left hand, a shield with the image of a severed head painted on it.

Sun Temple

Before you is a door of gold with the solar symbol stamped on it. You knock six times and the door swings open to reveal a stone circle made of six massive stone doorways—you have entered from a door in the west.

Within the circle, a great hexagram is traced in golden chips. At its center is a large stone altar—big enough for a person to lie upon. It has been covered with beaten gold. Upon the altar is a cross with a rose at its center. In the heart of the rose, there is an unearthly light.

It is a hot summer's day, and the bright Sun hangs high in the heavens. Your contacts will descend from the Sun and onto the altar.

In the east of the temple, there is a golden statue of a king on his throne. Under his feet is a lion that has a globe in its paws. The king holds a raven and is wearing a Calvary cross.

Jupiter Temple

Before you is a door made of tin with the astrological symbol for Jupiter stamped upon it. You knock four times and the door swings open to reveal a huge temple shaped like a pyramid. The walls of the temple are royal blue, and the floor is covered with rich purple carpet.

Four giant candles, which are placed in the corners of the pyramid on huge stands, light the room.

At the center of the temple is a cubic altar made of tin, but covered with a purple cloth. At its center is a simple candle placed in a tin dish that has been surrounded by the implements of royalty. In the east is a scepter of power; in the west, a crook; and in the north, an orb.

In the northwest of the temple, there is a door flanked by a silver-and-black pillar. Your contacts will come through this door.

In the east of the temple is a crystal statue of a crowned, naked man with his hands joined together and held before his face. He is on a four-legged throne, which is carried by four winged boys.

Saturn Temple

Before you is a door made of lead upon which you knock three times. The door opens to reveal a dark triangular pyramid.

The walls and floor are red-black, and three huge, black candles placed in the corners light the room. It would appear gloomy, but as you look closer you see that the carpet is made of tiny embroidered pictures of all of creation—like snowflakes, no design is the same. This idea continues on the walls so that it appears that every living creature has a representation in this place.

There is a lead altar in the center of the room that looks suspiciously like a coffin. On it is an hourglass and a cup. Inside the cup glows a bright, unearthly light that helps dispel the gloom.

In the southwest of the temple, there is a door flanked by a silver-and-black pillar. Your contacts will come through this door.

In the east is a lead statue of an old man clothed in black, with the face of a crow and camel's feet. He is sitting on a throne, and in his right hand is a scythe, and in his left hand, an arrow.

What Do Angels Look Like?

As I said earlier, the traditional image of angels as being men and women with wings belongs to the imaginations of medieval and Victorian artists and has been copied ever since. Angels are forces and have no more form than do electricity or gravity.

This state of affairs causes problems for us when we want to make contact with them. Humans see things in forms, even when they don't have form. Emotions, for example, have no form, yet we give them colors and even associate symbols like valentines to represent them. Provided we know that the form we build for our angel is not "real," it is alright for us to use forms to contact angelic presences.

Just as we did with the astral temples, it is possible to build the angels an appropriate form built of key symbols of their nature. Like the temples, it appears that it makes it easier for us to talk to them if they have the right form. This is an illusion. The form is to help us tune into them, rather than the other way around.

As you might expect, occultists have a lot of different ideas about the forms the different angels should take. There is the traditional approach and the Western Cabbalistic telesmatic approach (which was used by the Esoteric Order of the Golden Dawn).

The traditional approach gives human figures to some of the archangels. For example, Michael is represented as a red-winged soldier in medieval armor with an unsheathed sword. The traditional approach does not enable us to draw up clear images of some of the more obscure angels.

To solve this problem, the Esoteric Order of the Golden Dawn developed images based on the Hebrew letters that make up the angel's name, known as *telesmatic* images. Each Hebrew letter has an astrological or planetary attribution, as well as a meaning, which can be adapted to help draw an approximate picture of the angel. For example, Aleph means "Ox," so if an angel's name began with that letter it would either have the head of an ox, horns, or thick, bull-like features. Alternatively, the elemental or zodiacal attributions of the letters would be used so that Aleph would reflect the air element—wings or shafts of light colors.

The first letter is always attributed to the head, and the rest of the letters are evenly distributed over the rest of the body.

Agiel, whose name is made up of the letters Aleph, Gimel, Yod, Aleph, and Lamed, would have a winged head (Aleph, air); a blue Moon crescent headdress with a female face (Gimel, Luna); the body of a young woman (Yod, Virgo); large, golden wings from its lower back (Aleph, air); and well-proportioned limbs (Lamed, Libra).

The figures would be clothed in the colors that were appropriate from the spheres of the Tree of Life. Raphael, who is the archangel of Tiphareth, would be dressed in gold, while Gabriel, who is the archangel of the Yesod, would wear violet. We will look at the magical importance of these colors in chapter 7.

The Golden Dawn adepts were instructed to make these images as beautiful as possible. On its breast is the creature's sigil, and on its girdle is its name, with clouds placed beneath its feet.

This system works reasonably well. The problem is that since most archangels' and angels' names end with the suffix El or Yah, they all had wings and strong, evenly proportioned legs. Later Golden Dawn papers admitted this and worked on a slightly more elaborate system. For a start, they said to ignore the letters El or Yah at the end of an angel's name.

Rather than demanding that the images be made as beautiful as possible, they allowed composite images to be developed that were both animal and human. These were called *Kerubic figures*, and their colors were taken from the paths of the Tree of Life represented by the Hebrew letters.

Taking our example of Agiel, he would have the head of a golden eagle (Aleph, air); a blue, female face (Gimel, Luna); the body of a young woman (Yod, Virgo); and wear slate-gray robes.

To tell if your angel is male or female, count the number of letters that are male and how many are female. If there are more male letters, then the angel should be a man; if there are more female letters, it should be a woman. Using this method, Agiel is a female.

If there is an even number of male and female letters, the figure should be neither male nor female. If the letter calls for a face to be female on an otherwise male body, the figure should be a man's face with delicate, feminine features.

Here is a list of attributions based on those of the Golden Dawn. The colors listed are from the Windsor and Newton paint catalog.

Table 14
Descriptions of the angels derived from the Hebrew letters.

Aleph א: Spiritual, wings, epicene, an eagle, blue-emerald green, male.

Beth ב: Active and slight, mercurial, a caduceus, a monkey, gray, male

Gimel ג: Beautiful but changeable, a Moon disk, Moonlike features, camel, pale blue, female.

Daleth ד: Very beautiful and attractive. Full, rounded face and features, a rod of power, spring green, a dove, female.

He ה: Fierce, strong and fiery, an Egyptian looped cross (ankh), a ram, red flame, feminine.

Vau ו: Steady and strong, heavy and clumsy, shepherd's crook, a bull, warm olive, male.

Zayin ז: Thin, intelligent, possibly two heads or holding two swords or has two pairs of wings, sword, a bird, new yellow, female.

Cheth ח: Full face without much expression, armor or a chariot, a crab, rich bright russet, female.

Teth ט: Strong and fiery, a rose, a snake or lion, gray, female.

Yod י: Very white and delicate, lantern, a young woman, green-gray, female.

Kaph כ: Big and strong, a wheel, lightning, trappings of royalty, rich purple, male.

Lamed ל: Well proportioned, implements of justice (scales and sword), deep blue-green, female.

Mem מ: Reflective, dreamlike, a cup, epicene, a fish, deep olive-green, female.

Nun נ: Square and determined face, rather dark, a fish, a scorpion, dark brown, male.

Samekh ס: Thin, expressive face, a centaur, archer, green, male.

Ayin ע*:* Rather mechanical, predominating eyes, a goat, blue-black, male.

Pe פ: Fierce, strong, resolute, flames, lightning, iron, Venetian red, male.

Tzaddi צ: Thoughtful, intellectual, two vases, wings, a man, blue mauve, female.

Qoph ק: Rather full face (Moonlike), fluid, light translucent pink-brown, male.

Resh ר: Proud, dominant, Sun, a lion, rich amber, male.

Shin ש: Fierce, active, epicene, fire, scarlet flecked with gold, male.

Tau ת: Dark, a scythe, epicene, dark brown, male.

Making up images from these materials is a creative exercise that involves selecting parts and colors and rejecting others. Let us look at a couple more examples.

Raphael: Made up of the letters Resh and Pe (the rest are redundant). Male. Raphael would have the face of the Sun and would be wearing a rich, amber robe. His lower body would be covered in flames.

Graphiel: Made up of the letters Gimel, Resh, Aleph, Pe, and Yod. Female. She would have a pale, white face with blonde hair (I can't bear to see her with the face of a camel). She would have eagle wings from the top of her back and would wear a blue-emerald green robe. Her bottom half would be covered in flames and she would be wearing green-gray shoes.

Tzadqiel: Made up of the letters Tzaddi, Resh, Qoph, and Yod. Androgynous. It would have a male face that is thoughtful and intellectual. It would be wearing a bright, golden tunic with a Sun-disk medallion. It would wear shoes that are a light, translucent pink-brown mixed with gray-green.

Tiriel: Made up of the letters Teth, Yod, Resh, and Yod. Female. She would have the face of a lioness and the body of a young, delicate woman. She would be wearing a blue-green robe down to her feet, and have a belt with a large, golden Sun disk as a buckle.

After placing the name of the archangel, angel, intelligence, and spirit on a talisman, you are effectively sealing an agreement between you and the angel to work together toward a particular end. When you perform the consecration ceremony, you will be aware of the angel's force and know that it is working within your talisman. It also means that if you make a talisman for someone else, knowing the amount of work involved, you are unlikely to make one on a whim or just for cash.

---

1. Some believe that Samael has this task, but some occultists confuse him with a fallen angel with the same name. Golden Dawn scholar Adam Forrest has found that Golden Dawn leaders changed the good angel's name to Zamael to avoid confusion. The name Khamael, or Carmael, is sometimes used instead of Samael; but the name is the result of an error in transliteration and is meant to be Samael. See Chic and Sandra Tabatha Cicero, *Self-Initiation into the Golden Dawn Tradition* (Saint Paul, MN: Llewellyn Publishing, 1998) 158.

2. The Esoteric Order of the Golden Dawn taught that Camael was the head of the Order of Seraphim. As a result of this, they attribute Seraphim to the position of Geburah (Justice) on the Tree of Life; but the Seraphim stood in the presence of God and chanted, "Holy, Holy, Holy," which is a traditional position for angels of Kether or Daath. Camael has attributions to divine Justice (Geburah) and War, according to Eliphas Levi (*The History of Magic*, translated by Arthur Edward Waite, Rider, 1913)—the role of the powers is to make sure that Divine Justice is enforced, which is complementary to the role of Camael.

3. The clue is in the Hebrew spelling of Ashim (אשים): מ is attributed to water, י is attributed to earth, ש is attributed to fire, and א is attributed to air.

4. Maimondies put the Seraphim in this position.

5. The Zohar places the Elim in this position. Their name means "mighty ones."

6. Maimonides and the Golden Dawn put the Kerubim in this position.

7. I know of several magicians who have used this approach. They believed that the effort was a good technique to help them focus on the angel they were calling.

8. The term *pathworking* used to describe a series of meditations going up the paths of the Tree of Life. Now, however, it has come to mean any journey of the imagination designed to change a state of consciousness.

9. You should only look at an active flashing tablet. People will respond differently to this—some will become slightly disorientated, and others will not notice anything at all. If you experience the latter, do not stare at the tablet for longer than five minutes.

10. Agrippa said that this should be a dart, but, after some experimentation, I agree with Donald Tyson that this should be a flute. It is a subtly better symbol. See Henry Cornelius Agrippa, *Three Books of Occult Philosophy*, edited by Donald Tyson (Saint Paul, MN: Llewellyn Publishing, 1995) 38.

6

Snaring the Power of the Planets

In this chapter, we will be looking at the keys that magicians have used to harness planetary and angelic energy into their talismans. These include magic squares, sigils, and magical languages. We will also discuss the techniques of preparing the talisman at the correct time and designing them in the correct shape to attract the correct planetary energy.

Magical Languages

A magical language written on a talisman makes the talisman look obscure and mysterious; however, when the texts written in such languages are translated, they rarely reveal much in the way of information. Usually the talisman's intention, or talisman's purpose, is the only thing that is encrypted. An outsider would argue that there is no point writing something in an obscure talisman script, like Passing the River, when writing it in a modern language is just as effective.

There are several reasons why magical languages are useful in talisman making. The most obvious reason is that encoding the talisman's intention is vital. All magic works through a subtle play on the mind of the magician. Complex thought patterns are built on the astral level, which, by their nature, must manifest; however, that which is built by thought can also be destroyed by thought. If you tell someone your ritual intention, your thought structure is at his or her mercy. If the person chooses to laugh or deride your intention, your subjective belief in the power of your working could be shattered. Objectively, too, the person's derision may bring your thought structure crashing around your ears.

It is for this reason that secrecy was demanded among magicians. This applies to especially to talismans that are physical objects and are likely to be found, touched, and even studied by people who have the unconscious power to destroy them.

It has been my experience that even those who ask you to make a talisman may unconsciously seek to destroy its work. Many people approach someone who has magical skills out of desperation because they are unable to control their lives and they unconsciously block good things from happening to them. Their own negativity will stop a talisman working for them if they know its intention. Encryption prevents them knowing exactly how the intention will manifest and stops them from interfering in its work.

Another reason for using magical languages is that they have an inherent magical power. It is believed that an alphabet that is only used for magical or religious purposes carries a special "charge." It was for this reason that many Orthodox Jews were opposed to Israel using Hebrew as the state language. They feared that the language used to write all their holy texts would be contaminated by being used to write about mundane subjects.

A less obvious reason for using magical languages is that the letters develop a power in the minds of those who behold them. This is because the mind is confused by what it sees, assumes the letters are very powerful, and thus unconsciously gives the magician access to more magical energy. This is particularly true of the Enochian language, which was designed by the Elizabethan magician Dr. John Dee after a series of communications with angels.

Enochian was a language that no one could completely understand, and the fragments that Dee left us are fairly obscure. As such, when these fragments are used on talismans or spoken, they have a powerful magical effect. Unfortunately, some people have used this system unwisely and the power it has generated has unbalanced them, which is one of the reasons I do not recommend its use for beginners.

Easier to understand and use are the alphabets Passing the River, Theban, and Celestial (figures 9–11).

Theban is the easiest to use because it is a direct translation from English to Theban. Passing the River and Celestial are derived from Hebrew. The Hebrew-based words are written from right to left, with the magical script replacing the English letters. Although they do not have to be translated into Hebrew (unless you are very keen), there is a certain amount of letter substitution that has to be used, as there are some missing letters from both the Celestial and Passing the River scripts.

The easiest way to deal with this is to write out the intention of your talisman in English first:

"I ask the angel Raphael to heal my cat."

Then delete any letter *e*, replace any letter *c* with the letter *k*, and replace any letter *y* with the letter *i*:

"I ask th angl Raphal to hal mi kat."

Next, transliterate the letters into Hebrew equivalents. The letter *t* can be replaced by either Tau or Teth, and the letter *s* by Samekh or Shin. The letter *f* should be replaced with either an *s* or a *ph* (Pe). Letter combinations can also be changed if you wish: *gh* can be replaced by Gimel, *dh* by Daleth, *kh* by Kaph, *aa* by Ayin, *sh* by Shin, and *th* by Tau. The vowel *a* is represented by Aleph, *i* by Yod, and *o*, *u*, and *v* by the letter Vau. Our example ends up looking like this:

Yod, Aleph, Samekh, Kaph, Tau, Aleph, Nun, Gimel, Lamed, Resh, Aleph, Pe, Aleph, Lamed, Tau, Vau, He, Aleph, Lamed, Mem, Yod, Kaph, Aleph, and Tau.

Then reverse the text:

Tau, Aleph, Kaph, Yod, Mem, Lamed, Aleph, He, Vau, Tau, Lamed, Aleph, Pe, Aleph, Resh, Lamed, Gimel, Nun, Aleph, Tau, Kaph, Samekh, Aleph, and Yod.

Finally, replace the letters with the relevant script (in this case, Celestial), and the result is:

ᄀᄎᄃᄼᄼ᎐ᄎ ᄁᄀᄀ᎐ᄎᄀᄎ ᄀ᎐ᄀᄼᄎ ᄀᄃᄓᄎᄼ

Figure 9. Celestial alphabet.

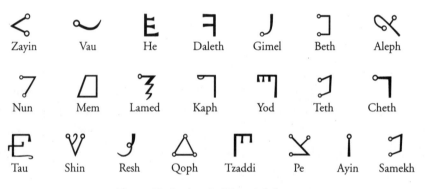

Figure 10. Passing the River alphabet.

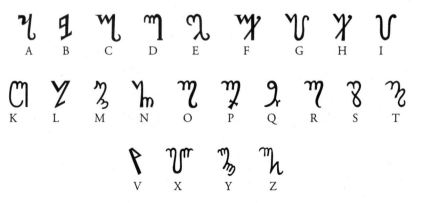

Figure 11. Theban alphabet.

Magic Squares

Magic squares use the power of numbers and the Hebrew letters with which they are associated to attract planetary power onto a talisman.

Agrippa pointed out that the ancients, particularly the Pythagoreans, considered numbers to be the key to understanding the universe. Every number meant something to them, and every mathematical act was considered a holy act.

Planetary forces had numbers that later would be attributed to the Cabbalistic Tree of Life. Mars would be five; Venus, seven; the Sun, six; Saturn, three; the Moon, nine; and Jupiter, four.

Magic squares are grids of numbers that equal the same number whether they are added horizontally, vertically, or diagonally (figures 13–19). The mathematics behind this is described in appendix V of the Donald Tyson edition of Agrippa's *Three Books of Occult Philosophy*. This information, however, is not necessary to learn, since magicians from the fifteenth century onward tended to copy the same seven squares for each of the planets mentioned in Agrippa's book.

Although there are other magic squares that have been used, these "authorized" versions have subtle and tested powers. As I have stated throughout this book, it is important to understand what these squares mean before trying to build talismans around them.

The secret is to look at the numbers and the Hebrew letters associated with them. For example, figure 12 is the Saturn square:

4	9	2
3	5	7
8	1	6

Figure 12. The Saturn square.

It encloses the number five. We know that five is the number of Mars (the planet attributed to energy and motion), so we can assume that the energy of Saturn encloses all action. However the energy remains and is in a position to be tapped. The top row is comprised of the numbers four, nine, and two. Four is the number of stability and Jupiter, nine is the number of the Moon and the unconscious, and two is the number of reflection and the unconscious. By meditating on all these things, connections will start to emerge, making the magic square real to your unconscious, magical mind.

One magical school interprets magic squares by using Tarot cards and the wealth of associations connected with these to bring forth associative ideas to the waking mind. I have also provided the Hebrew letters associated with the numbers, which are helpful in unlocking ideas. If the top row of our Saturn square is made up of Resh (face), Teth (a snake), and Beth (a door), it is possible to use these symbols to unlock hidden meanings and make the square come alive for you.

Once these squares become a reality in your consciousness, they will be seen as an interrelating grid of planetary power. When they are placed on a talisman, they will almost glow with raw planetary power.

4	9	2		ר	ט	ב
3	5	7		ג	ה	ז
8	1	6		ח	א	ו

Figure 13. The Saturn magic square.

4	14	15	1		ד	יד	טו	א
9	7	6	12		ט	ז	ו	יב
3	11	10	8		ה	יא	י	ח
16	2	3	13		יו	ב	ג	יג

Figure 14. The Jupiter magic square.

11	24	7	20	3
4	12	25	8	16
17	5	13	21	9
10	18	1	14	22
23	6	19	2	15

יא	כב	ז	כ	ג
ד	יב	כה	ח	יו
יז	ה	יג	כא	ט
י	יח	א	יד	כב
כג	ו	יט	ב	יה

Figure 15. The Mars magic square.

3	32	3	34	35	1
7	11	27	28	8	30
19	14	16	15	23	24
18	20	22	21	17	13
25	29	10	9	26	12
36	5	33	4	2	31

ו	לב	ג	לד	לה	א
ז	יא	כו	כח	ח	ל
יט	יד	יו	יה	כג	כד
יח	כ	כב	כא	יז	יג
כה	כט	י	ט	כו	יב
לו	ה	לג	ר	ב	לא

Figure 16. The Sun magic square.

22	47	16	41	10	35	4
5	23	48	17	42	11	29
30	6	24	49	18	36	12
13	31	7	25	43	19	37
38	14	32	1	26	44	20
21	39	8	33	2	27	45
46	15	40	9	34	3	28

כב	מז	יו	מא	י	לה	ר
ה	כג	מח	יז	מב	יא	כט
ל	ו	כד	מט	יח	לו	יב
יג	לא	ז	כה	מג	יט	לז
לח	יד	לב	א	כו	מד	כ
כא	לט	ח	לג	ב	כז	מה
מו	יה	מ	ט	לר	ג	כח

Figure 17. The Venus magic square.

8	58	59	5	4	62	63	1
49	15	14	52	53	11	10	56
41	23	22	44	45	19	18	48
32	34	35	29	28	38	39	25
40	26	27	37	36	30	31	33
17	47	46	20	21	43	42	24
9	55	54	12	13	51	50	16
64	2	3	61	60	6	7	57

ח	נח	נט	ה	ד	סב	סג	א
מט	יה	יד	נב	נג	יא	י	נו
מא	כג	כב	מד	מה	יט	יח	מח
לב	לד	לה	כט	כח	לח	לט	כה
מ	כו	כז	לז	לו	ל	לא	לג
יז	מז	מו	כ	כא	מג	מב	כד
ט	נה	נד	יב	יג	נא	נ	יו
סד	ב	ג	סא	ס	ו	ז	נז

Figure 18. The Mercury magic square.

37	78	29	70	21	62	13	54	5
6	38	79	30	71	22	63	14	46
47	7	39	80	31	72	23	55	15
16	48	8	40	81	32	64	24	56
57	17	49	9	41	73	33	65	25
26	58	18	50	1	42	74	34	66
67	27	59	10	51	2	43	75	35
36	68	19	60	11	52	3	44	76
77	28	69	20	61	12	53	4	45

לז	עח	כט	ע	כא	סב	יג	נד	ה
ו	לח	עט	ל	עא	כב	סג	יד	מו
מז	ז	לט	פ	לא	עב	כג	נה	יה
יו	מח	ח	מ	פא	לב	סד	כד	נו
נז	יז	מט	ט	מא	עג	לג	סה	כה
כו	נח	יח	נ	א	מב	עד	לד	סו
סז	כז	נט	י	נא	ב	מג	עה	לה
לו	סח	יט	ס	יא	נב	ג	מד	עו
עז	כח	סט	כ	סא	יב	נג	ד	מה

Figure 19. The Moon magic square.

Planetary Seals

Planetary seals are a way of refining and focusing the energy generated by magic squares. They are drawings that are made using the magic square, linking the energy into a clear pattern. This pattern, if drawn correctly, links all the numbers into an intense unity: each line and circle of a seal passes through every square in the grid.

There is a problem, however; the magicians who used magic squares have passed to us the rules for making planetary seals, but not all the planetary seals obey them. The Mars, Venus, and Moon seals do not touch all the squares in the magic square.

There could be many reasons for this. The most obvious is that when Agrippa's printers published his work, they made mistakes on the illustrations. None of the drawings require significant changes to make them "correct"—some lines are missing and the proportion of the lines on others is slightly incorrect. An accident of the plate maker's hand could account for these errors. In the days of early print making, such problems did bedevil magical texts.

The next possibility is that the mistakes were deliberate. The three planetary seals involved are important from the perspective of the talisman maker. Talismans for love (Venus) and the courts and battle (Mars) were a part of a magician's stock and trade. They were also those that had the greatest potential for being used with black magic. The Moon seal, if used in a particular way, can provide a huge amount of personal power. I think it is likely that Agrippa "tweaked" these seals' designs so that the unscrupulous or ignorant could not use them.

He left us the Saturn, Jupiter, and Sun seals with which to demonstrate the principles of seal design. Although it is possible to wreck havoc with these seals, their planetary energies require a more experienced magician to evoke them. Mars is the easiest energy to contact, followed closely by the Moon energy, and then Venus energy.

Since Agrippa published his book, most magicians through the ages have copied his versions. Their squares may have worked, but if they had corrected them, their talismans may have been more effective.

Following Agrippa's principles I have restored the planetary seals to what I believe might be their original forms, while maintaining the shapes suggested by him (figures 20–29). Using the talisman-testing techniques described later in this book, the new versions provided a noticeable increase in the amount of planetary energy.

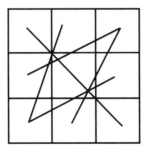

Figure 20. The seal of Saturn.

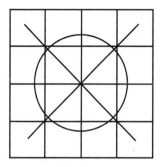

Figure 21. The seal of Jupiter.

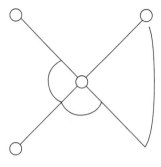

Figure 24. The seal of Mars, according to Agrippa.

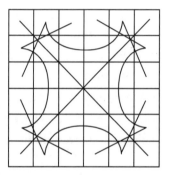

Figure 22. The seal of the Sun.

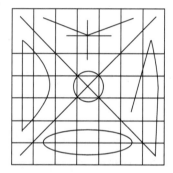

Figure 25. The suggested seal of Venus.

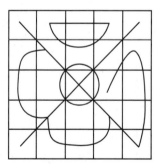

Figure 23. The suggested seal of Mars.

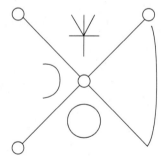

Figure 26. The seal of Venus, according to Agrippa.

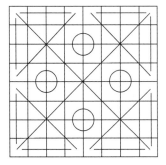

Figure 27. The seal of Mercury.

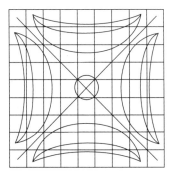

Figure 28. The suggested seal of the Moon.

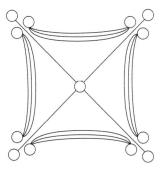

Figure 29. The seal of the Moon, according to Agrippa.

Sigils of Angels and Spirits

Sigils are angelic and spiritual signatures of approval. Like planetary seals, they are derived from the power of the magic square; but, unlike the seals, they only use certain numbers from which they gain their power. These numbers are derived from the Hebrew letters of their names when placed on a magic square. For example, for the name of the spirit of Jupiter, Hismael, a line would have to pass through the letters He, Samekh, Mem, Aleph, and Lamed on the magic square of Jupiter. This would work well except for the fact that there is no letter Mem or Lamed in the Jupiter square.

Agrippa used a further method of coding called Aiq Beker, or Cabbalah of Nine Chambers (figure 30). This enables you to replace a letter that is missing from the magic square with another that is present. The letters are assigned so that their numbers are similar to the Hebrew numerical values.

300 30 3	200 20 2	100 10 1
ש ל ג	ר כ ב	ק י א
600 60 6	500 50 5	400 40 4
ם ס ו	ך נ ה	ד מ ת
900 90 9	800 80 8	700 70 7
ץ צ ט	ף פ ח	ן ע ז

Figure 30. Aiq Beker substitution chart.

Firstly, you convert all the letters in the Hebrew name to numbers and then reverse them (because we are using Hebrew). Taking our Hismael example (השמאל in Hebrew), this would be Lamed (30), Aleph (1), Mem (40), Samekh (60), and He (5).

Next, you reduce all the numbers so that they are less than the number of cells in your magic square (in this case, the magic square is Jupiter, which has sixteen squares). In this case, we would reduce Lamed to three, Mem to Four, and Samekh to six. Each angelic name has to add up to a number that is significant for the magic square that you are using. Each magic square has three significant numbers—the number of its cells, the sum of each row, and the sum of all the cells in the square. For this reason, some letter values are fudged so that the names actually add up to the right number. Sometimes the values of the letter combination "Yod Aleph" are sometimes added together to make eleven. Other fudges include linking Shin and Mem into single squares.

In our Jupiter example, the letters that have a numeric value higher than sixteen are Lamed (30), Mem (40), and Samekh (60). If we look at the Aiq Beker chart, we can see that Samekh (60) can be reduced to Vau (6), Mem (40) to Daleth (4), and Lamed (30) to Gimel (3).

Hismael can thus be written on a Jupiter talisman using the numbers three, one, six, and five, or the letters Gimel, Aleph, Mem, Vau, and He. Once the lines are drawn, they are sometimes shown with either a circle or a line at each end. *The name begins with a circle and ends with a line.* If a line has to enter the same box twice, a crook or a wave is placed there.

Hismael's sigil would look like this:

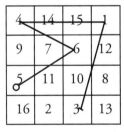

Figure 31. Hismael's sigil.

Here are the other seals:

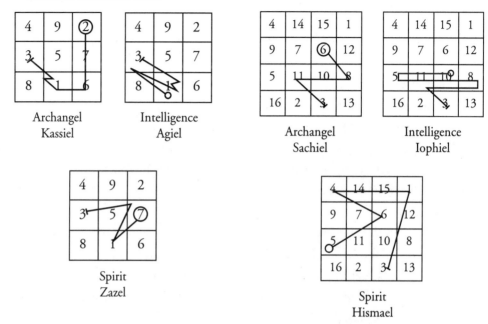

Archangel
Kassiel

Intelligence
Agiel

Archangel
Sachiel

Intelligence
Iophiel

Spirit
Zazel

Spirit
Hismael

Figure 32. Sigils for the angels and spirits of Saturn.

Figure 33. Sigils for the angels and spirits of Jupiter.

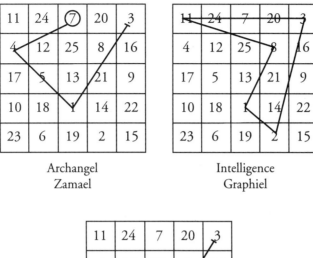

11	24	⑦	20	3
4	12	25	8	16
17	5	13	21	9
10	18	1	14	22
23	6	19	2	15

Archangel
Zamael

11	24	7	20	3
4	12	25	8	16
17	5	13	21	9
10	18	1	14	22
23	6	19	2	15

Intelligence
Graphiel

11	24	7	20	3
4	12	25	8	16
17	5	13	21	9
10	18	1	14	22
23	6	19	2	15

Spirit
Bartzabel

Figure 34. Sigils for the angels and spirits of Mars.

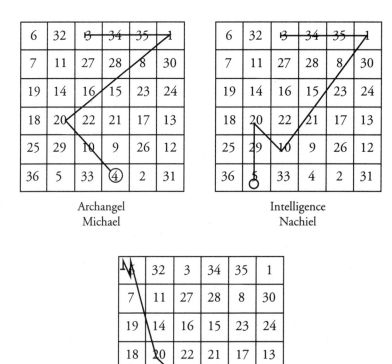

Figure 35. Sigils for the angels and spirits of the Sun.

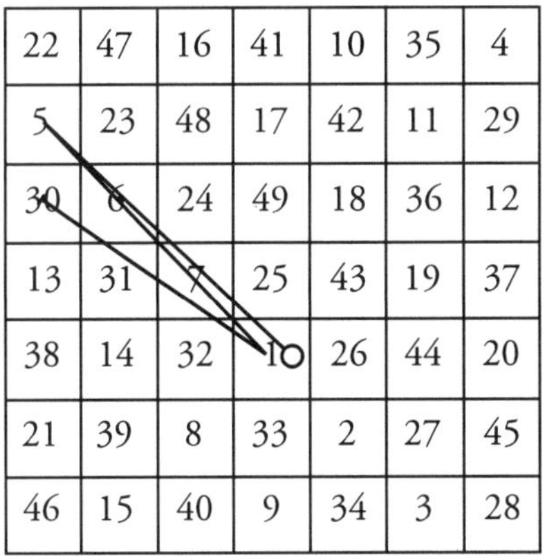

22	47	16	41	10	35	4
5	23	48	17	42	11	29
30	6	24	49	18	36	12
13	31	7	25	43	19	37
38	14	32	1	26	44	20
21	39	8	33	2	27	45
46	15	40	9	34	3	28

Archangel
Anael

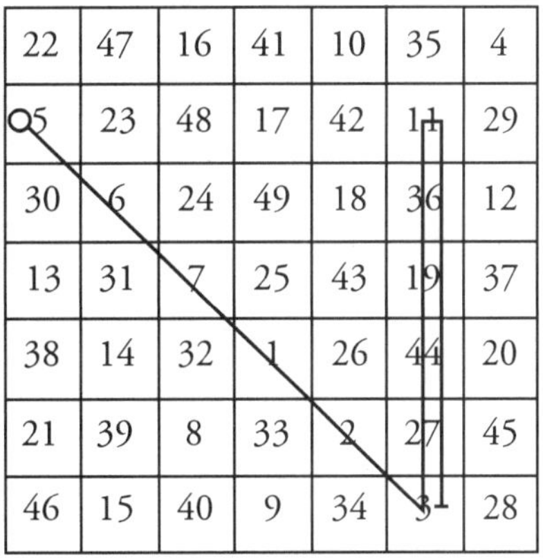

22	47	16	41	10	35	4
5	23	48	17	42	11	29
30	6	24	49	18	36	12
13	31	7	25	43	19	37
38	14	32	1	26	44	20
21	39	8	33	2	27	45
46	15	40	9	34	3	28

Intelligence
Hagiel

22	47	16	41	10	35	4
5	23	48	17	42	11	29
30	6	24	49	18	36	12
13	31	7	25	43	19	37
38	14	32	1	26	44	20
21	39	8	33	2	27	45
46	15	40	9	34	3	28

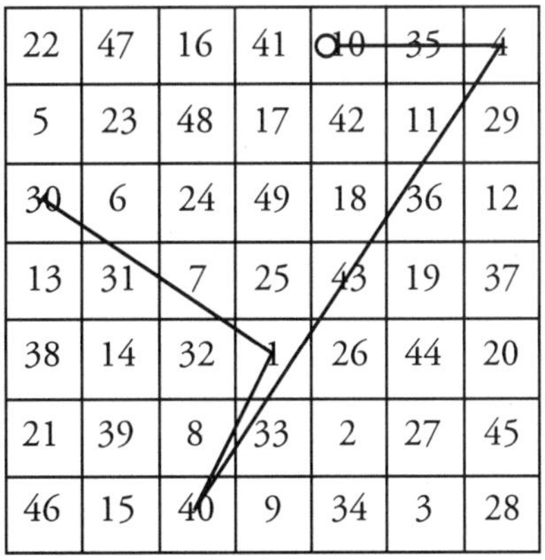

Spirit
Qedemel

Figure 36. Sigils for the angels and spirits of Venus.

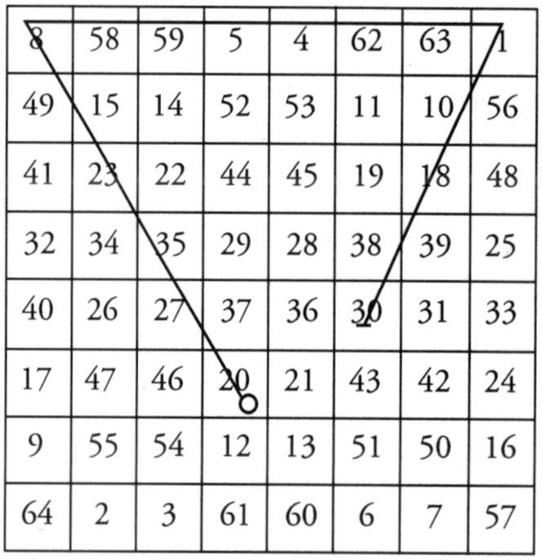

8	58	59	5	4	62	63	1
49	15	14	52	53	11	10	56
41	23	22	44	45	19	18	48
32	34	35	29	28	38	39	25
40	26	27	37	36	30	31	33
17	47	46	20	21	43	42	24
9	55	54	12	13	51	50	16
64	2	3	61	60	6	7	57

Archangel
Raphael

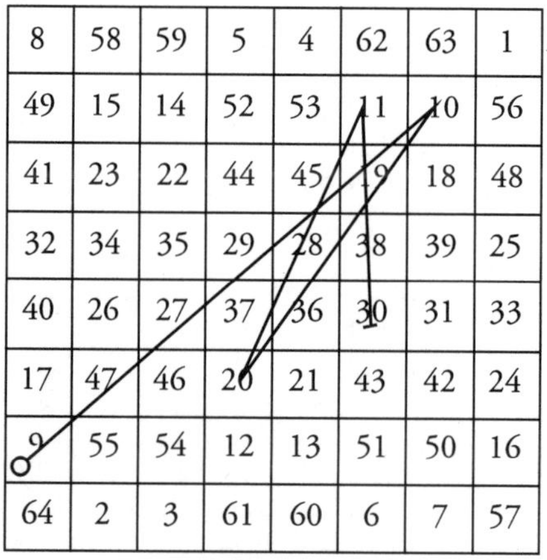

8	58	59	5	4	62	63	1
49	15	14	52	53	11	10	56
41	23	22	44	45	19	18	48
32	34	35	29	28	38	39	25
40	26	27	37	36	30	31	33
17	47	46	20	21	43	42	24
9	55	54	12	13	51	50	16
64	2	3	61	60	6	7	57

Intelligence
Tiriel

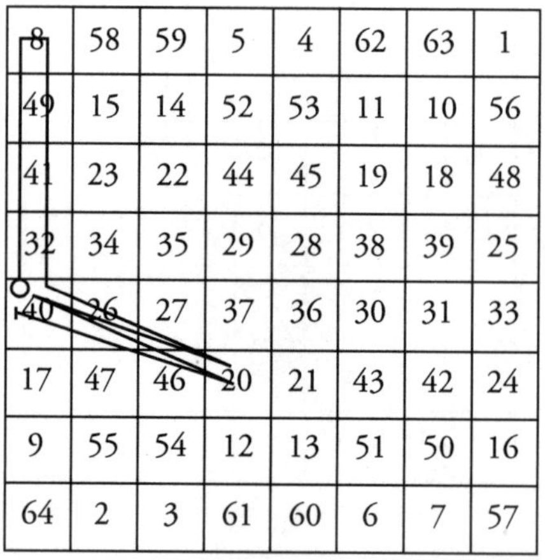

8	58	59	5	4	62	63	1
49	15	14	52	53	11	10	56
41	23	22	44	45	19	18	48
32	34	35	29	28	38	39	25
40	26	27	37	36	30	31	33
17	47	46	20	21	43	42	24
9	55	54	12	13	51	50	16
64	2	3	61	60	6	7	57

Spirit
Taphthartharath

Figure 37. Sigils for the angels and spirits of Mercury.

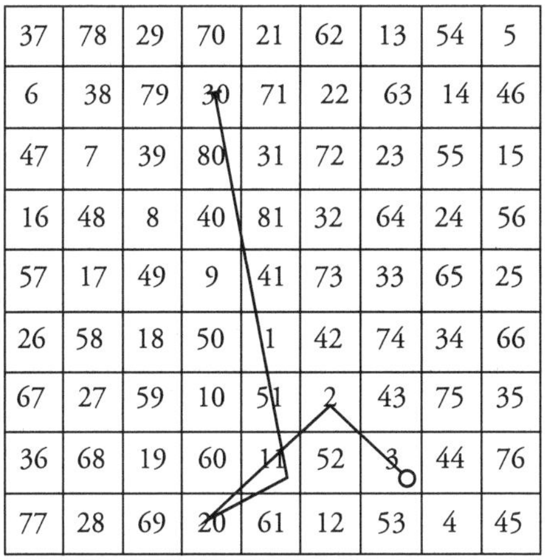

37	78	29	70	21	62	13	54	5
6	38	79	30	71	22	63	14	46
47	7	39	80	31	72	23	55	15
16	48	8	40	81	32	64	24	56
57	17	49	9	41	73	33	65	25
26	58	18	50	1	42	74	34	66
67	27	59	10	51	2	43	75	35
36	68	19	60	11	52	3	44	76
77	28	69	20	61	12	53	4	45

Archangel
Gabriel

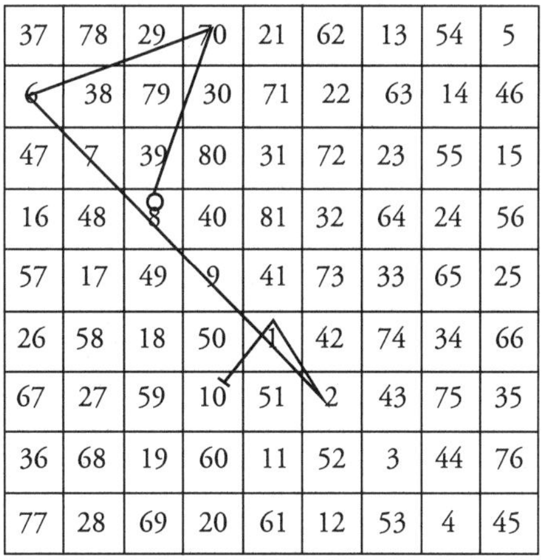

37	78	29	70	21	62	13	54	5
6	38	79	30	71	22	63	14	46
47	7	39	80	31	72	23	55	15
16	48	8	40	81	32	64	24	56
57	17	49	9	41	73	33	65	25
26	58	18	50	1	42	74	34	66
67	27	59	10	51	2	43	75	35
36	68	19	60	11	52	3	44	76
77	28	69	20	61	12	53	4	45

Spirit
Chashmodai

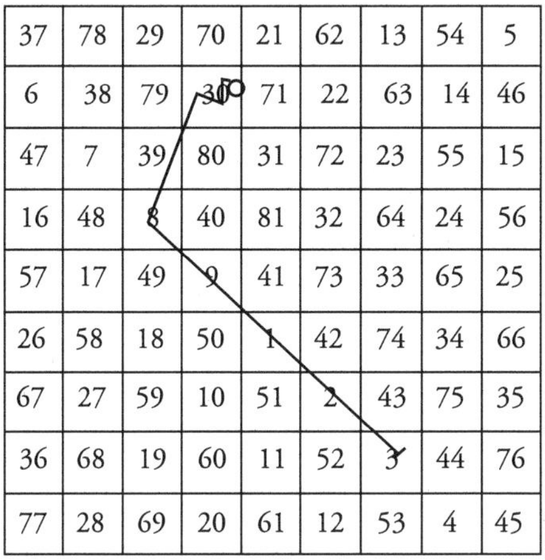

37	78	29	70	21	62	13	54	5
6	38	79	30	71	22	63	14	46
47	7	39	80	31	72	23	55	15
16	48	8	40	81	32	64	24	56
57	17	49	9	41	73	33	65	25
26	58	18	50	1	42	74	34	66
67	27	59	10	51	2	43	75	35
36	68	19	60	11	52	3	44	76
77	28	69	20	61	12	53	4	45

Intelligence
Malkah be Tarshisim ve-ad
Ruachoth Schechalim

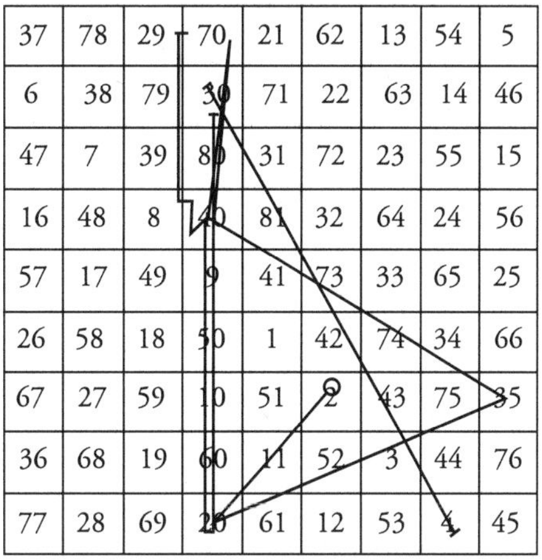

37	78	29	70	21	62	13	54	5
6	38	79	30	71	22	63	14	46
47	7	39	80	31	72	23	55	15
16	48	8	40	81	32	64	24	56
57	17	49	9	41	73	33	65	25
26	58	18	50	1	42	74	34	66
67	27	59	10	51	2	43	75	35
36	68	19	60	11	52	3	44	76
77	28	69	20	61	12	53	4	45

Spirit of Spirits
Schad Barschemoth ha Shartathan

Figure 38. Sigils for the angels and spirits of the Moon.

Use of Sigils

There are two ways of using magic squares, planetary seals, and sigils. The first is to physically place them on your talisman. In this way, the magic squares and sigils would be like a signature on the bottom of a formal document.

There is another way of using them, however, that has never been released outside of esoteric schools. First, you draw or paint a large version of the magic square, preferably using the flashing colors given in chapter 7. Place the object or talisman on top of the magic square and carefully draw the outline of the seal of the planet in the air over the relevant squares. Then invoke the angel, intelligence, or spirit that you wish to call and draw the outline of the sigil over the relevant squares.

This will invoke the planetary force from the tablet and then fuse it into the sigil of the angel or spirit. The object or talisman will be caught in the energy that emerges from the magic square and tuned to its particular flavor. The design of the talisman and any consecration ritual will assist in keeping this power in the object and allow it to radiate outward.

Planetary Hours and Days

Each planet has an hour during each day and a day of each week when it is more powerful than usual. It therefore makes sense, when constructing talismans, to use these times to entrap more planetary energy into your talismans.

Planetary days are simply the days of the week. Sunday is the day of the Sun; Monday; the Moon; Tuesday, Mars; Wednesday, Mercury; Thursday, Jupiter; Friday, Venus; and Saturday, Saturn.

You should begin working on your talisman on the most appropriate planetary day and during the correct planetary hour (and preferably finish making it during that hour). Likewise, any consecration and empowerment rituals should be started on the correct planetary day and during the correct planetary hour. If you are drawing the talisman on a computer, you should print it out during the correct planetary hour.

Calculating planetary hours by hand is not that simple. You need to know the exact time that the Sun rose and set, which can be found on the Internet or by consulting a newspaper.

Then, starting from the time the Sun rose and ending at the time it set, you divide the day into twelve equal parts. Note that during certain times of the year, planetary hours last longer than sixty minutes, and at other times of the year, they last less than sixty minutes.

Consulting table 15, you can ascertain the planet that is most powerful during each of the planetary hours. For example, on Tuesday during the tenth planetary hour, the strongest planetary power is Venus. If you were consecrating or making a Mars talisman, the best time to do so would be during the hours of Mars and on the day of Mars; that is, either at sunrise or during the eighth planetary hour on Tuesday.

There is a similar technique used to find the planetary hours of the night. This is based on the times of sunset and sunrise of the next day. For more information on how to calculate planetary hours by hand, using perpetual planetary hour tables, or using a planetary hour computer program, see Maria Kay Simms' book *A Time for Magick: Planetary Hours for Meditations, Rituals & Spells*.

Table 15
Daytime planetary hours.

Division of Day	Sun	Mon	Tues	Wed	Thurs	Fri	Sat
1	Sun	Moon	Mars	Mercury	Jupiter	Venus	Saturn
2	Venus	Saturn	Sun	Moon	Mars	Mercury	Jupiter
3	Mercury	Jupiter	Venus	Saturn	Sun	Moon	Mars
4	Moon	Mars	Mercury	Jupiter	Venus	Saturn	Sun
5	Saturn	Sun	Moon	Mars	Mercury	Jupiter	Venus
6	Jupiter	Venus	Saturn	Sun	Moon	Mars	Mercury
7	Mars	Mercury	Jupiter	Venus	Saturn	Sun	Moon
8	Sun	Moon	Mars	Mercury	Jupiter	Venus	Saturn
9	Venus	Saturn	Sun	Moon	Mars	Mercury	Jupiter
10	Mercury	Jupiter	Venus	Saturn	Sun	Moon	Mars
11	Moon	Mars	Mercury	Jupiter	Venus	Saturn	Sun
12	Saturn	Sun	Moon	Mars	Mercury	Jupiter	Venus

Table 16
Nighttime planetary hours.

Division of Night	Sun	Mon	Tues	Wed	Thurs	Fri	Sat
1	Jupiter	Venus	Saturn	Sun	Moon	Mars	Mercury
2	Mars	Mercury	Jupiter	Venus	Saturn	Sun	Moon
3	Sun	Moon	Mars	Mercury	Jupiter	Venus	Saturn
4	Venus	Saturn	Sun	Moon	Mars	Mercury	Jupiter
5	Mercury	Jupiter	Venus	Saturn	Sun	Moon	Mars
6	Moon	Mars	Mercury	Jupiter	Venus	Saturn	Sun
7	Saturn	Sun	Moon	Mars	Mercury	Jupiter	Venus
8	Jupiter	Venus	Saturn	Sun	Moon	Mars	Mercury
9	Mars	Mercury	Jupiter	Venus	Saturn	Sun	Moon
10	Sun	Moon	Mars	Mercury	Jupiter	Venus	Saturn
11	Venus	Saturn	Sun	Moon	Mars	Mercury	Jupiter
12	Mercury	Jupiter	Venus	Saturn	Sun	Moon	Mars

7

Color Magic and Talismans

Early talismans, which have survived the passage of time, are colorless (although some Hebrew talismans have red- or blue-colored beads attached to them to provide additional protection); however, color was considered an important magical tool in the more esoteric schools. As long ago as the time of the Middle Kingdom of ancient Egypt, specific colors were attributed to the different gods, and any deviation from these attributions was not permitted.

Occult tradition states that the ancients knew, as we do now, that color was light vibrating at different frequencies, each of which corresponded to a particular planetary influence. While Agrippa and other medieval magicians did not discuss the uses of color, they did provide planetary color scales, but left it up to the magician to find a proper use.

The Esoteric Order of the Golden Dawn made color magic into an elaborate science. Color was an obvious part of the Order's ceremonies and other magical work.[1] Each magical implement was painted in a color that corresponded to its particular function and planetary association.

At the grade Adeptus Minor, the Golden Dawn student was taught some 140 magical colors, each connected to the Tree of Life, that were linked to powerful planetary and astrological forces.

When applying these colors to talismans, the technique was to paint the background in the color of the force required and the divine names and sigils in a complementary, "flashing" color. A solar talisman would be painted yellow, while all the sigils, divine and angelic names, and magical images were painted in purple. A simple object hoping to attract a Mars force would be colored scarlet-red and have a green Mars (♂) symbol painted on it. The paint colors were carefully mixed until they appeared to "flash" with magical energy.

This is often as far as people go with using the Golden Dawn color magic system, but often what they are missing is the opportunity to use color to tune their talismans even further and create very focused talismans of power.

The Colors

Before looking at the various techniques of color magic, let us look at the colors used by the Golden Dawn. They took Aggripa's color attributions for the planets and expanded them further, adding colors of the spheres and paths of the Tree of Life.

Earlier in this book, we saw that each sphere has a planet attributed to it; for example, Jupiter is attributed to Chesed. By painting a talisman in a color that is attributed to a sphere on the Tree of Life, you are also painting it in an appropriate planetary color.[2] The associations of each sphere included all the attributions and vices of the planets. Order, planning, rulership, and financial gain are attributed to both Chesed and Jupiter.

There is a different color for all ten spheres on the Tree of Life and the twenty-two paths that connect them.[3] These connection paths are halfway houses between the spheres and what they represent. For example, the midway point between Mercy (Chesed) and Justice (Geburah) is the nineteenth path, which is represented by the letter Teth ט, which, you remember, means "snake."

Cabbalists said that the spheres on the Tree of Life made up the first ten paths, and the twenty-two connecting paths were numbered from eleven to thirty-two.

In the Golden Dawn system, each path had a Tarot trump and a planetary power assigned to it that gave symbolic clues to its meaning. This makes it possible to make planetary or zodiacal talismans using the colors of the paths—perhaps by placing the appropriate Tarot card in the center of the talisman. There are a number of publishers that print microsized Tarot cards quite cheaply, which would work well. If you make such a talisman, I would suggest that you use the divine name and angelic names attributed to the appropriate planet or sign of the zodiac.

For example, a Jupiter talisman would have Key 10, the Wheel of Fortune in the center (along with the intention), the angel Jupiter (Sachiel), the archangel Chesed, (Tzadqiel), the divine name Chesed (El), and a big Hebrew letter Kaph.

There were different scales of color for the divine (Atziluth), archangelic (Briah), angelic (Yetzirah), and material levels (Assiah). These were known as the King (Atziluth), Queen, (Briah), Prince (Yetzirah), and Princess (Assiah) scales. They were based on the Windsor and Newton paintbox and are official Golden Dawn colors.

Table 17
Colors through the Cabbalistic worlds.

Path number/ name and Tarot key	Divine level King scale	Archangelic level Queen scale	Angelic level Prince scale	Earth level Princess scale
1. Kether	Diamond light (Brilliance)	White brilliance	White brilliance	White flecked with gold
2. Chockmah	Soft blue	Gray	Bluish mother of pearl	White flecked with red, blue yellow
3. Binah	Crimson	Black[4]	Dark brown	Gray flecked with pink
4. Chesed	Deep violet	Blue	Deep purple	Deep azure flecked with yellow
5. Geburah	Orange	Scarlet-red	Bright scarlet	Red flecked with black
6. Tiphareth	Clear, pink rose	Yellow (gold)	Rich salmon	Golden amber
7. Netzach	Amber	Emerald	Bright yellow-green	Olive flecked with gold

Path number/ name and Tarot key	Divine level King scale	Archangelic level Queen scale	Angelic level Prince scale	Earth level Princess scale
8. Hod	Violet-purple	Orange	Red russet	Yellow-brown flecked with white
9. Yesod	Indigo	Violet	Very dark purple	Citrine flecked with azure
10. Malkuth	Yellow	Citrine, olive, russet, black	Four colors flecked with gold	Black rayed with yellow
11. Aleph, Fool	Bright-pale yellow	Sky blue	Blue-emerald green	Emerald flecked with gold
12. Beth, Magician	Yellow	Purple	Gray	Indigo rayed with violet
13. Gimel, High Priestess	Blue	Silver	Cold, pale blue	Silver rayed with sky blue
14. Daleth, Empress	Emerald green	Sky blue	Early spring green	Bright rose of cerise rayed with pale yellow
15. He, Emperor	Scarlet	Red	Brilliant flame	Glowing red
16. Vau, Hierophant	Red orange	Deep indigo	Deep, warm olive	Rich brown
17. Zayin, Lovers	Orange	Pale mauve	New yellow	Red-green inclined toward mauve

Path number/ name and Tarot key	Divine level King scale	Archangelic level Queen scale	Angelic level Prince scale	Earth level Princess scale
18. Cheth, Chariot	Amber	Maroon	Rich, bright russet	Dark green-brown
19. Teth, Strength	Greenish yellow	Deep purple	Gray	Red amber
20. Yod, Hermit	Yellowish green	Slate gray	Green	Gray plum
21. Kaph, Wheel of Fortune	Violet	Blue	Rich purple	Blue rayed with yellow
22. Lamed, Justice	Emerald green	Blue	Deep blue-green	Pale green
23. Mem, Hanged Man	Deep blue	Sea green	Deep olive-green	White flecked with purple, like mother of pearl
24. Nun, Death	Green-blue	Dull brown	Very dark brown	Indigo brown-black
25. Samekh, Temperance	Blue-green	Yellow	Green	Dark, vivid blue
26. Ayin, Devil	Indigo	Black	Blue-black	Cold, dark gray, nearly black
27. Pe, Tower	Scarlet	Red	Venetian red	Bright red rayed with emerald
28. Star, Tzaddi	Violet	Sky blue	Blue mauve	White tinged with purple

Path number/ name and Tarot key	Divine level King scale	Archangelic level Queen scale	Angelic level Prince scale	Earth level Princess scale
29. Qoph, Moon	Ultra violet crimson	Buff flecked with silver-white	Light, translucent pink-brown	Stone
30. Resh, Sun	Orange	Gold yellow	Rich amber	Amber rayed with red
31. Shin, Judgement	Glowing scarlet-orange or citrine, olive, russet black	Vermillion or amber	Scarlet flecked with gold or dark brown	Vermillion flecked with crimson or black and yellow
32. Tau, Universe	Indigo or white, merging gray	Black or deep purple	Blue black or seven prismatic colors violet outside	Black rayed with blue or white, red, yellow, blue and black
Daath[5]	Lavender	Gray white	Pure violet	Gray flecked with gold

A magician could use these colors to target certain forces on different levels. If, for example, the magician wanted to build a talisman that only worked with archangelic forces, he or she would color it entirely in the Queen scale. If it the talisman was to work only with planetary angels, the Prince scale would be used.

If the talisman's target was to work on the intellect or emotions (which correspond to the Yetzaratic level), the magician would use the Prince scale; if it was for actions relating to spiritual development, the magician would use the Queen scale; and if it was for physical well-being, the Princess scale.

It is unlikely that a talisman would be made using only the King scale, although one could perhaps be made for spiritual revelation or vision. Talismans that only target one of the four worlds were rarely made, as the magician usually wanted a result on all levels.

Talisman featured a divine name (King scale), an archangel (Queen scale), and an angel (Prince scale), to control either a spirit or physical target (Princess scale); so they were potentially very colorful.

Golden Dawn adepts in Whare Ra whom I have spoken to tend to make their talismans out of Queen scale colors;[6] in fact, Queen scale is the most popular color scheme among many post–Golden Dawn groups. Perhaps this is because this level is the most successful at providing general-purpose talismans that can provide satisfactory results on all levels.

Flashing Colors

There are two types of flashing colors—active and passive. The most common flashing color used on a talisman is the active color. This is when your background color is the energy you want to attract, and the complementary color (sometimes called the *activator*) is placed on top.

For example, if you were creating a Jupiter talisman for financial well-being in the Queen scale, you would use blue (Chesed)[7] as your background color and orange as the activator. The orange would "flash" and activate the blue so that it would continuously attract the Jupiter-Chesed energy.

What if you wanted to banish something from your life? For example, say you had a phobia you wanted to get rid of. Normally you would construct a lunar talisman, because the Moon controls habit patterns; however, the last thing you would want to do is further empower your phobia by directing more lunar force into it. Instead, you would want the lunar power removed from the habit pattern.

In these circumstances, you would use the passive flashing color. This is the reverse of the active flashing color. Your talisman's background would be painted in a composite color and the activator would be painted in the color of the sphere on the Tree of Life. In the case of fixing a phobia, you would build a yellow talisman with violet activating letters.[8]

True flashing colors require careful mixing. I list here twelve of the main colors and their flashing or complementary colors to give you a rough idea of what the flashing color is. You will know when you have the correct combination because the colors will start to jazz your eyes or seem to move or vibrate when the artwork is shaken.

Table 18
Flashing colors.

Color	Flashing color
Red	Green
Red-orange	Blue-green
Orange	Blue
Yellow-orange	Blue-violet
Yellow	Violet
Yellow-green	Red-violet
Green	Red
Blue-green	Red-orange
Blue	Orange
Blue-violet	Yellow-orange
Violet	Yellow
Red-violet	Yellow-green

Flashing Tablets

Flashing tablets are an excellent way of attracting planetary force to an inanimate object using color. They are disks about the size of a small dinner plate, which are painted in the Queen scale. Upon them is drawn a single planetary symbol in an appropriate flashing color. Saturn would be red-black[9] with a white ♄; Jupiter would be blue with an orange ♃; Mars would be scarlet with a green ♂; the Sun would be yellow with a violet ☉; Venus would be green with a red ♀ (figure 39); and the Moon would be violet with a yellow ☽.

The function of a flashing tablet painted in active flashing colors is to take the white light of the environment and convert it into blind planetary force. This force radiates outward from the tablet and can be seen by someone who is sufficiently psychic. Exposure to this energy affects matter subtly and draws it slowly toward the influence of the tablet's planetary force.

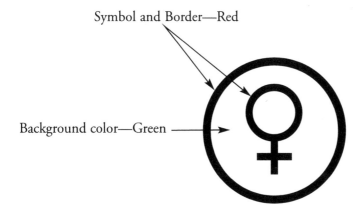

Symbol and Border—Red

Background color—Green

Figure 39. Flashing tablet of Venus.

The upshot of a tablet's activity is that if an object is placed on the tablet for a period of time, it will start to glow with planetary force. This planetary force will not stay in the object for longer than about a month. While the object remains charged, it will be easier to consecrate and improve its long-term effectiveness.

A tablet painted in passive flashing colors will slowly banish planetary force from the material object. This is useful if you want to remove the planetary energy, but also want to maintain the planet's angelic influence over your intention. Banishing tablets can also be used to deconsecrate active talismans over a period of time.[10]

A flashing tablet can be made of wood, cardboard, or even paper. A circular wooden chopping board, which can be bought cheaply from most supermarkets, makes an ideal flashing tablet. These boards have a circular groove cut into them that makes an ideal rim between the border and the flashing part of the tablet.

You can paint the active colors on one side of the tablet, and the passive colors of the planet on the other side.

The storage of flashing tablets is important because they leak planetary energy and can attract unpleasant beings if left lying around. Fortunately, since they require light to work, they are deactivated if left in darkness. A box or bag that does not admit any light will insulate a flashing tablet from causing any harm. Unlike a talisman, a well-made flashing tablet can last a lifetime. If it ever needs to be replaced, it should be completely destroyed.

To charge an object by using a flashing tablet, place the item on a stand about an inch above the flashing tablet. The stand will allow light to pass under the object and activate the flashing tablet. For best results, expose the tablet to sunlight during the day and to electric light during the night. If this level of concentration of light is achieved, the material object will be fully charged by the flashing tablet within twenty-four hours in the summer, and forty-eight hours in the winter. If it is left in normal light during the day and in darkness during the night, it will take seven to ten days to achieve the same charge.

Flashing Squares

Flashing squares are recent additions to the armory of color magic and have recently been the subject of successful magical experiments by modern magicians. Although flashing squares work in a fashion similar to flashing tablets, a flashing square provides a much more active force (some magicians call this an *initiatory force*) that is pointed toward the divine beings and angels being used in a talisman.

A flashing square is a planetary magicsquare drawn on a ten-inch-square piece of cardboard or wood. There are two schools of thought as to the colors that can be used. Some people use Agrippa's planetary color system (using silver for Mercury), while others prefer the Golden Dawn system. The background of the magic square should always be painted in the color of the planet, while the numbers, or letters, and the grid should be painted in the activating flashing colors.

A flashing square can be constructed either using Hebrew or the numbers in figure 13. I find that I get better results using Hebrew.

As I mentioned in the last chapter, flashing squares can be used to force planetary force into sigils and shapes that remain in the aura of a living talisman.

They should not be used in place of a flashing talisman, but rather as a complementary part of the process. The flashing tablet energizes the object, while the flashing square initiates it to its purpose by impregnating it with divine energy. Together, they make extremely powerful talismans.

Like flashing tablets, it is possible to make "negative" flashing squares. Like the tablets, these are painted in the banishing flashing colors. Flashing squares, however, are less useful than flashing tablets. When constructing a talisman, you always want the power of the angels and spirits, but a banishing tablet will remove these influences. Banishing tablets are useful as part of a deconsecrating ritual, where they can be used to banish angelic and spirit influences from an object. They are also useful in certain kinds of exorcism where a planetary spirit is causing problems.[11]

Both forms of flashing squares are tools that are used as part of ceremonial magic rituals. They do not require a long period of time to work. They should be used in light, but an object only needs to be placed upon them for the duration of the ritual.

The storage of flashing squares is a little more complicated, as they are not just activated by light but maintain their energy levels through the power of the letters on them. For this reason, they should be kept in a silk bag or a lead box.

Further Tuning of a Talisman Using Color

Cabbalists say that there is a Tree in every sphere on the Tree of Life. This means that each sphere has its own Malkuth, Yesod, Hod, Netzach, Tiphareth, Geburah, Chesed, and so on. Practically speaking, it means that there are subtle differences in each of the spheres that correspond to others and take on part of their nature. For example, when Geburah (Mars) appears as part of the other spheres of the Tree of Life, it brings an element of discipline or justice to them. The love of Netzach becomes "tough love" (Geburah in Netzach), Geburah in Hod develops military science, and Geburah in Chesed indicates merciful justice.

This information can be used to tune talismans more accurately. For example, if you wanted to make a talisman to heal a damaged romantic relationship, normally you would make a Netzach (Venus) talisman; however, it would actually be better to make a Tiphareth (Sun) in Netzach (Venus) talisman. If you wanted to improve communication with a loved one, you would use Hod (Mercury) in Netzach (Venus). If you wanted financial well-being that resulted in you receiving cash, you would make a Malkuth (Earth) in Chesed (Jupiter) talisman; but if you wanted financial well-being that manifested in a house appearing for you, then you would use a Binah (Saturn) in Chesed (Jupiter) talisman.

There is little difference between these types of talismans other than the color, and even that is not particularly marked. The difference lies in the mind of the magician making the talisman, which has been focused by the process of mixing the colors.

When painting the talisman, make nine daubs of the main color of the sphere in your mixing bowl. Then add a single daub of the color of the other sphere, and mix them together. For example, if we were using the Queen scale, our Tiphareth in Netzach talisman would have nine daubs of green paint and a single daub of yellow. A Mercury in Netzach talisman would have nine parts green with one part orange.

This becomes slightly more complicated when making talismans that use spheres like Malkuth, where there are four colors. Colors of nonplanetary talismans of earth[12] (perhaps Tiphareth of Malkuth) are achieved by using the nine-part ratio in all four colors; however, if you are looking at Malkuth in Chesed, the best approach is to paint your Chesed color as normal and then paint a Malkuth sphere over the top with heavily watered-down paint. This should be watered down to the point that it gives a slight ghosting effect, hinting at Malkuth colors.

Coloring Thought Forms

In the last chapter we described techniques for visualizing angels. Color is an important issue in building up thought forms as it gives astral power to the thought form you want to build.

The colors of thought forms vary in accordance with their natures. An archangel will be colored using the Queen scale; an angel, the Prince scale; and a spirit, the Princess scale.

Thought forms will also receive the colors of their spheres. Angels and spirits attributed to Mars will use the colors of Geburah or the fifth path, while those of the Moon will be dressed in the colors of Yesod or the ninth path. Martial spirits could be dressed in the colors of the path of Pe, while lunar spirits could be dressed in the colors of the path of Gimel.

Based on this color scheme, Raphael, the archangel of Tiphareth, would wear yellow robes; Michael, the angel of the Sun, and Nakhiel the intelligence would wear a rich, salmon color. Sorath the spirit would wear gold-amber.

If you wish, it is possible to get quite detailed in the way color is used with thought forms. One technique involves using color to indicate the ability of an angel or spirit to walk between the four worlds.

Thought forms of archangels are crowned by a halo of King scale color. Paint the heads and necks in Queen scale colors; torsos and legs in Prince scale colors; and feet in Princess scale colors.

Thought forms of Angels and intelligences would have halos of Queen scale; heads, torsos and legs in Prince scale; and feet in the Princess scale.

Thought forms of spirits would have halos in Prince scale colors, and the rest would be in Princess scale colors.

Using this system, Raphael would have a halo of clear, pink rose, a face and neck of yellow, a rich, salmon-colored robe, and golden-amber shoes. Michael and Nakhiel would have yellow halos, salmon-colored faces and robes, and golden-amber shoes. Sorath would have a salmon-colored halo and wear gold-amber.

---

1. For color illustrations of these implements, see Chic and Sandra Tabatha Cicero, *Creating Magical Tools* (Saint Paul, MN: Llewellyn Publishing, 1999).

2. The spheres on the Tree of Life have wider meanings that simply planetary meanings. By using such colors, you are making a talisman that has access to slightly more than just planetary associations.

3. There were also colors for the mystical sphere of Daath (which was not a traditional sphere on the Tree of Life) and two different colors for paths 31 and 32.

4. Modern Golden Dawn initiates have differing views on the Queen scale color Binah. In private correspondence, Tabatha Cicero told me that "this is one of those times when I part from certain aspects of Golden Dawn tradition. All the Supernals are *achromatic*—white, gray, and black—they are without color in the normal sense of the word 'color.' All the other spheres are *chromatic* (with color). This is one of those things that sets the Supernals apart from the rest of the Tree. Red-black would not be achromatic."

5. Daath is not a path and therefore does not have a number.

6. Whare Ra was a Golden Dawn Order based in Havelock North, in Hawkes Bay, New Zealand. It was established just after the first world war and closed in 1979.

7. You could also use the colors of the Kaph path.

8. This is using the Queen scale; however, if you wanted to be really focused, you would be better off making this particular talisman, which is connected with the emotions (Yetzirah), in Emperor scale, which would be a dark yellow with dark-purple lettering.

9. See footnote 4.

10. Note that this will not exorcise a talisman after use. A deconsecration ceremony is still required to break the associations with the angels and planetary spirits; but after this is performed, the passive flashing tablet will remove any trace of planetary force from the material component, enabling it to be destroyed safely.

11. These are sometimes created by high-level magical workings and, as such, are extremely rare and require a special type of magical expertise, both to create the problem in the first place and to get rid of it. These skills include the ability to find the sigil of the rogue spirit in question in order to gain control of it.

12. See chapter 9.

8

Drawing Talismans

In previous chapters, we have looked at the many magical components that go into making the material components of talismans. We have also discussed different techniques to make those components as magically real as possible. In this chapter, we will be bringing all this information together to manufacture a material shell for the creatures of energy we will be creating.

The Body of the Talisman

Throughout this book, you have heard me describe talismans as *living creatures*. This is because they have elements in common with living beings. I am not using the biological definition of life, which requires an ability to breed and breathe. Talismans are not sentient in any scientific sense, as they are totally focused on their "life goal." The talisman has no more sentience than a computer running a program, and if it appears to provide inspiration, then it is because it is connected to divinity.

Talismans are similar to the Jewish magical tradition's concept of a golem. They are objects of matter that have been animated by a human using divine force.

- A talisman has a material body that reflects certain aspects of the divine.

- A talisman has an influence on several levels of reality.

- A talisman has a life goal and dies when that goal is completed.

- A talisman has a degree of intelligence with which to bring about its life goal.

- A talisman has enough energy to bring about its life goal.

- A talisman has an aura.

Occult philosophy says that for a body to be a vessel for divine power, it should be a physical reflection of that divinity. The closer an object reflects deity, the more deity will shine through it. In the Judeo-Christian mythology, humans are important in the cosmic scheme of things because "God made man in his own image." Because we were made in the deity's image, we can be perfect vessels for its expression.[1]

Like humanity, a talisman should be "made in the image" of the divine forces that it represents; however, this is not to be taken too literally, or talismans would be scale models of the planets. The "image" we are hoping to capture is like a mathematical formula that describes the force. A talisman should be like an astrology chart that captures through symbols the personality of planetary forces.

Jewish talismans and Greek katadesmoi were constructed on the basis of faith in a divine being. In a time when the view of the universe was based entirely on faith, these requests on paper and lead sheet were enough of a microcosm to reflect the universe. The more scientific minds of later periods, however, demanded that more information be placed within the body of the talisman.

Historically, talismans were made of certain metals with planetary affinities to help capture planetary forces. Saturn talismans were made of lead; Jupiter talismans were made of tin; Mars talismans, iron; Sun talismans, gold; Venus talismans, copper or brass; and Moon talismans, silver. Talismans made for Mercury, which is a fluid metal, were usually made of silver.

The medieval magical texts also talk of talismans being made on paper and virgin parchment, painted on wood and stones, or made of metals that were unconnected to the planets. It was believed that the planetary colors, magical formulas, divine names, and sigils more than compensated for not having the correct metal.

Most modern talismans are made of paper, cardboard, or painted wood. This is not only due to cost (the price of a four-inch gold disk is extremely high), but because these mediums allow the most flexibility and allow for flashing colors to be painted on them. If a mistake is made, the half-finished talisman can simply be thrown away and restarted without too much expense.

Talismanic Shapes

We have not yet discussed the shapes of talismans in much detail. Basic talismans were traditionally circles or squares, as these shapes provided the most room on which to inscribe text or draw sigils. The Esoteric Order of the Golden Dawn hinted to its members that shapes could be used to attract planetary influence and provided a set of attributions for different shapes.[2] However, I have found no evidence that the Golden Dawn attempted to apply this information to talismans, and tended to follow the same model used by Francis Barrett.

Further research work carried out within other esoteric Orders has revealed that talismans made in accordance with the correct planetary shape can hold charges that are between 5 and 10 percent higher.[3]

Since anything that enhances a talisman's performance should be a feature of its design, this book is the first to recommend publicly that the esoteric teaching on polygons and polygrams be incorporated into talisman design.

Polygons contain energy, while polygrams (or stars) expand the energy outward. If you wanted to build a talisman for an individual, you would use a polygon; but if you wanted to make one for a region, you would use a polygram. A pentagram (a star) would be used to protect a school from burglars, whereas a pentagon (a polygon) would protect an individual from harm.

Star-shaped talismans are good for helping solve national problems. They would be used if you wanted a talisman to reduce infant mortality or move to find a cure for a type of cancer. You should not think that you are too "small" or inexperienced to attempt making talismans to solve such huge national problems. Such issues start to be solved when one person decides to correct them. While a talisman may not solve the problem overnight, it will bring about some of the steps for a solution, which will ultimately correct the problem. Bare in mind, however, that such talismans often work through their maker, so do not be surprised if, after making a talisman to help the homeless, you are inspired to volunteer to work at your local homeless shelter.

Saturn and Jupiter talismans are two exceptions to the rules on polygons and polygrams. This is because their shapes are both stars and polygons—Saturn is a triangle and Jupiter is a square. The way around this problem is to use the triangle and the square as your star talismans, and to enclose the triangle or square in a circle for polygon talismans.

Generally, you will be making talismans that are polygons. These are formed by drawing a circle on a piece of paper or cardboard and then using a protractor to divide the circle by the number of points on the polygram. The points are then connected by lines to make an enclosed figure.

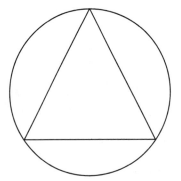

Figure 40. Talisman shape for Saturn (Binah).

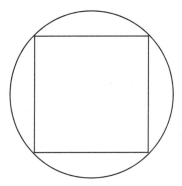

Figure 41. Talisman shape for Jupiter (Chesed).

A triangle within a circle is attributed to Saturn and Binah on the Tree of Life. The corners of the triangle are made at 120-degree intervals around the circle.

A square in a circle is attributed to Jupiter and Chesed on the Tree of Life. The corners of the square are made at 90-degree intervals around the circle.

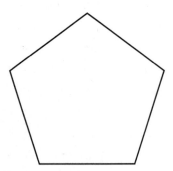

Figure 42. Talisman shape for Mars (Geburah).

The pentagon is attributed to Mars and Geburah on the Tree of Life. The corners of the pentagon are made at 72-degree intervals around the circle used to proportion its shape.

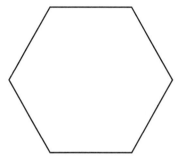

Figure 43. Talisman shape for the Sun (Tiphareth).

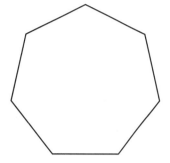

Figure 44. Talisman shape for Venus (Netzach).

The hexagon is attributed to the Sun and Tiphareth on the Tree of Life. The corners of the hexagon are made at 60-degree intervals around the circle used to proportion its shape.

The heptagon is attributed to Venus and Netzach on the Tree of Life. The corners of the heptagon are made at 51.42-degree intervals around the circle used to proportion its shape.

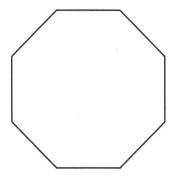

Figure 45. Talisman shape for Mercury (Hod).

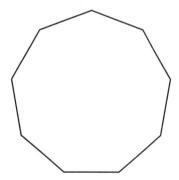

Figure 46. Talisman shape for the Moon (Yesod).

The octagon is attributed to Mercury and Hod on the Tree of Life. The corners of the octagon are made at 45-degree intervals around the circle used to proportion its shape.

The enneagon is attributed to the Moon and Yesod on the Tree of Life. The corners of the enneagon are made at 40-degree intervals around the circle used to proportion its shape.

Basic Talismans

We will be looking at more complicated talismans in a moment, but simple talismans can be designed using the information already provided. Having decided which planet and sphere on the Tree of Life to use, you would then select a shape. You would cut this out of appropriately colored cardboard (see the previous chapter) roughly four to six inches in size.

If it were a Sun talisman, you would cut out a hexagram. Ideally, you would do this on a Sunday at sunrise.

Within the shape, about half an inch away from the edge of the talisman, you would draw a smaller version of the shape so that it forms a border. Your Sun talisman would look like figure 47:

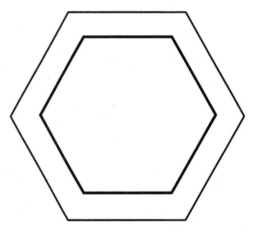

Figure 47. Basic shape of a Sun talisman.

Next, you would write the divine name for the sphere of the Tree of Life on the top of the border and the name of the archangel for that sphere on the bottom of the border (figure 48). These should be written in Hebrew, which can be found in chapter 5, and they should be written in the flashing color of the cardboard. Note that it is the archangel of the *sphere* that you want, not the archangel of the *planet*. In the

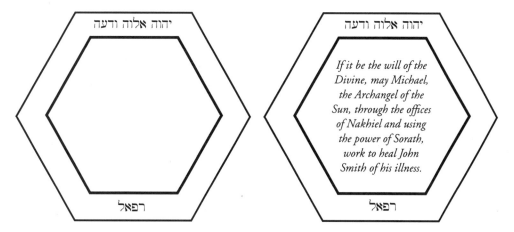

Figure 48. Putting on the divine names.   **Figure 49.** Placing the intention.

case of your Sun talisman, the divine name would be Yhvh Eloah Vedaath אלוה ודעה
יהוה, and the archangel would be Raphiel רפאל.

Next, within the center of the talisman, you would write your intention (figure 49). This should begin with the phrase "If it be the will of the Divine." Basically, this phrase removes you from many karmic implications if the action you are taking is wrong or may interfere with another person's life pattern. The next part of the intention should ask the archangel of the planet to work through the intelligence and spirit of the planet to achieve the goal. Ideally, the intention should be written in one of the magical scripts like Angelic, Theban, or Passing the River. In figure 49, I have written the intention in English to provide an example of an intention.

Underneath the intention, you should place the symbol of the planet. In the illustration, it is the Sun. Above it should be a sigil that is designed by taking the initials of the person for whom the talisman is being made and merging the letters together (figure 50). In this case, the person is John Smith and the letters *J* and *S* are merged into a composite figure.

יהוה אלוה ודעה

If it be the will of the Divine, may Michael, the Archangel of the Sun, through the offices of Nakhiel and using the power of Sorath, work to heal John Smith of his illness.

רפאל

Figure 50. Placing planetary and personal sigils.

Turning the talisman over, you would draw an equal-armed cross on the back (figure 51). This serves to seal the power into the talisman and prevent it from leaking away.

This completes the building of your basic talisman. All that remains to be done is to consecrate it using one of the systems in the next chapter. This type of talisman is easy to make and can be just as powerful as some of the more complicated talismans I will be describing later. What makes talismans more powerful is the ability of the magician to interact with the entities described in the talisman. A magician who has visited with the entities that are mentioned on their talismans and who has their approval for their manufacture will always make more successful talismans, however basic their designs may be.

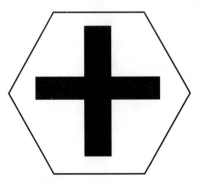

Figure 51. The back of the talisman.

Advanced Talismans

Building the body of a more advanced talisman requires all the components that we have discussed thus far. It also requires knowledge of the four-worlds principle that we discussed in chapter 1. An advanced talisman is more complicated and a more accurate picture of the universe. In theory, this would give it more power, as additional symbols are called into play and more of the universe is depicted. In practice, this is not always the case, as the ability of magicians to comprehend what they are looking at is in proportion to their skill and experience. There is also more practical work required beforehand, such as meeting the various angels and spirits whose names will appear on the talisman.

There are two types of advanced talismans. The first is the sort of talisman depicted by Francis Barrett and used by the Esoteric Order of the Golden Dawn. These can be found in chapter 2 and are in essence a larger, round version of the simple talisman we just discussed. The difference is that there is much more information placed on the advanced talismans.

In the center of one of the disks is the magic square of the planet, the sign of the planet, and the appropriate Hebrew name of God. Around the circumference is the number of the spirit of the planet, another divine name, and the name of the intelligence of the planet.

In the center of the second disk is the seal of the planet, the sign of the planet, and the sigil, or signature, of the intelligence.

In addition to Barrett's talisman formula, the adepts of the Esoteric Order of the Golden Dawn added flashing colors to the mix. The examples of Golden Dawn talismans that I have seen have also included carefully drawn pentangles from the Key of Solomon or magical images of the planets on some of the underside faces.

So what should a talisman look like?

- A talisman should have an appropriate shape.

- A talisman should reflect the four levels of the universe.

- A talisman should contain the divine names from the spheres on the Tree of Life.

- A talisman should contain the names of the archangel of the appropriate sphere on the Tree of Life, and the names of the intelligence and the spirit.

- A talisman should contain the symbol and seal of the appropriate planet.

- A talisman should contain an intention that draws together all the names and seals.

- A talisman should contain a link between the talisman and the person or object for whom the talisman is designed.

- A talisman should be appropriately colored.

Making a talisman reflect the four-level nature of the universe is simple. You divide the talisman into four levels: the outer ring is the divine level, the next is the level of archangels, the next is the level of angels, and the remaining level is the realm of spirits and earth (figure 52). It is a diagram of the universe seen through the eyes of Deity. It is a bit like looking down the wrong end of a telescope, where God is the closest and the material is the furthest away; and it depicts how power flows down the levels to focus on the material portion of the talisman.

Each of the four levels should be appropriately colored. The divine level should be painted in the King scale, the archangelic level in the Queen scale, the Angelic level in the Emperor scale, and the material level in the Empress scale.

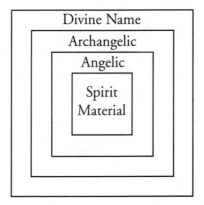

Figure 52. Outline of the four-worlds talisman.

If the talisman is to be an invoking talisman, each level should be painted in active flashing colors; if it is to be a banishing talisman, passive flashing colors should be used. For example, an active Mars talisman (pentagon) would have an outer ring of orange, a ring of scarlet red, another of bright scarlet, and an inner part of red flecked with black (figure 53). A passive banishing Mars talisman would have an outer ring of blue, and then green, blue-green, and green flecked with white.

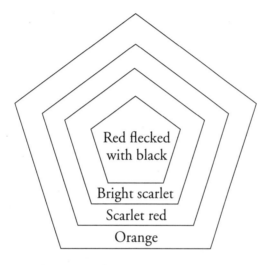

Figure 53. Colors active on a Mars talisman.

The letters of each of the divine names and the names of the spirit should be painted in flashing colors to the background.

If you wish to place any relevant Bible verses on the talisman, you can place them in flashing letters on the same level as the divine name. These verses can either be complete, or written in Notarikon. I included a list of these in chapter 3; however, it is always best to search for your own verses using a good interlinear Hebrew-English Bible.[4]

The archangelic level contains the archangel of the sphere on the Tree of Life as well as the archangel of the planet.

The next level contains the divine name of the intelligence of the planet, or the intelligence of intelligences of the Moon.

The final level is a little more complicated because it has to contain a lot of information. Firstly, it should contain the name of the planetary spirit. Next, it should contain a planetary square with the seal of the planet correctly drawn on top of it. Then you should write the intention in a magical script, a symbol of the planet, and finally a sigil for the person for whom the talisman is intended. If you are particularly artistic, you could draw a picture of the magical image of the planet.

What you now have is an image of the person's sigil surrounded by a number of planetary symbols. These symbols permeate the sigil with their power. They are controlled by the words of the intention and the great weight of magical energy pouring down upon them from the other three levels of creation.

With this picture it is easy to imagine that all planetary energy, which is symbolically depicted as bearing down on the person's sigil, would place the person under a considerable amount of magical pressure. In fact, the image on the talisman is engineered to make the person's sigil look like Atlas bearing the weight of the world on his shoulders; that is, the person's sigil is at the center of tremendous planetary pressure. It is this pressure that causes magical change.

During the next phase of talisman making, when it is consecrated and bought to life, the spirits behind the talisman will use this symbolic picture as their reason for living and work to make what is essentially a picture a reality.

During my own experience in making talismans of this type, I have developed tweaks to their basic design that improve their overall efficiency. Firstly, I always include the divine name יהוה, or YHVH, in white letters in the divine name sector of every talisman. I break the letters up so that the yod is always in the top right-hand corner: the first He is top left, the Vau is bottom left, and the second He is on the bottom right. This divine name is one of the most important magical names of deity in the Judeo-Christian tradition, particularly among Rosicrucians who attributed many important occult teachings to it.

The reason I place a divine name on talismans is because each of the letters of the name is attributed to an element: Yod is attributed to fire, the first He is water, Vau is earth, and the last He is air. It is through the division of deity into these four elements and their subsequent interaction that enables all activity in the universe to take place. They also provide a measure of divine protection for the maker of the talisman and for the person for whom the talisman is intended. The Rosicrucians had a saying, "May you be protected by the shadow of the wings of Jehovah," that gives a rough idea of the protective nature of this name.

Once יהוה has been added, a lightning flash should be painted in white from each of the four letters through each of the four worlds until they point to the last world (figure 54). A lightning flash is a powerful symbol of the divine powers of heaven quickly moving to earth. I find that by using a lightning flash in conjunction with the divine name, you speed up the process of making your intention manifest.

Lastly, you should turn the talisman over and insert a special cross on the back. This cross (figure 55) is borrowed from John Dee's Seal of Truth. The seal was one of the most important pieces of Dee's magical equipment because it protected his crystal ball from spirits that would not tell the truth.[5] As such, this cross was placed on the bottom to protect the seal from the evil powers of the earth and to keep the magical powers of the seal of truth from dissipating.

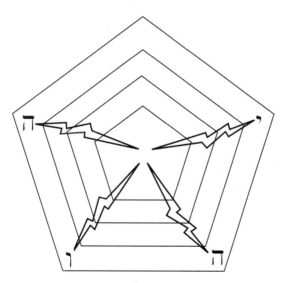

Figure 54. The lightning flash on a four-worlds talisman.

The letters AGLA are Notarikon for a phrase that means "Thou art mighty forever, O Lord." It is used as a divine name of exorcism of the earth. The cross and the name will provide the same type of protection for any talisman and prevent any energy from leaking into the earth and thus weakening it. A completed four-worlds talisman is shown in figure 56.

Figure 55. John Dee's cross.

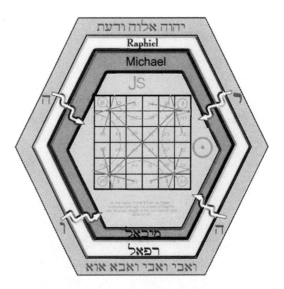

Figure 56. A completed four-worlds talisman.

Earth Talismans

Earth, or geomantic, talismans work in a totally different way from other talismans. Unlike other forms of talismans that call power from the heavens, geomantic talismans draw their power from the Earth.

All planetary influence falls directly on the earth where it mixes with earth energy that comes from the center of the planet. This planet-earth hybrid energy can be contacted by using geomantic symbols.

Technically, geomancy is a technique of divination where you poke holes in the earth. These holes are added together to make symbols, much in the same way that coin tossing or yarrow sticks are used to construct I Ching trigrams. The use of geomantic symbols has been a feature of talisman making for hundreds of years. In order to understand the fortunetelling system of geomancy fully, you should read Chic and Sandra Tabatha Cicero's *Self-Initiation into the Golden Dawn*.

Geomantic figures have found their way onto ordinary planetary talismans, where they are usually placed in the same sector as the spirits; however, this is a confusion of two very different types of energy. Ordinary planetary talismans draw power down from the planets, while the geomantic figures draw planetary power up from the Earth. On a purely geomantic talisman, this earth-planetary force can be controlled properly with appropriate divine names and sigils; whereas on a mixed talisman, the earth component is uncontrolled and often ineffective.[6]

As a general rule, you would only build an earth talisman if you wanted a result to happen on earth. These are the sort of talismans that are manufactured to gain money, a car, a house, physical health, or a job. They are not as effective at obtaining spiritual development, correcting emotional problems, healing when the problem is caused by unresolved emotions, or intellectual issues like passing exams or correcting memory.

Table 19
The sixteen geomantic symbols.

Tristitia
Saturn

Aquisitio
Jupiter

Fortuna Major
Sun

Albus
Mercury

Carcer
Saturn

Laetitia
Jupiter

Fortuna Minor
Sun

Conjunctio
Mercury

Via
Moon

Puer
Mars

Amissio
Venus

Caput Draconis
North Node

Populus
.Moon

Rubeus
Mars

Puella
Venus

Cauda Draconis
South Node

For talismans, the dots that make up the various tetragrams are joined to make specific shapes. All these shapes are placed on a talisman (figure 57).

You will notice that there are two geomantic shapes for each of the planetary energies. This means, for example, that at least two shapes would have to be placed on an earth talisman.

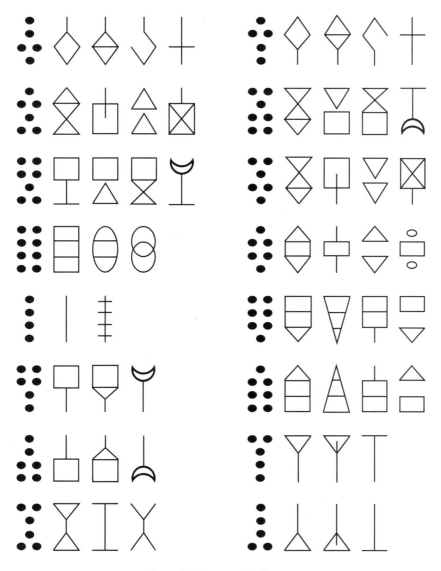

Figure 57. Geomantic talismans.

Sigils of Spirits on Earth Talismans

The planetary spirits have different sigils when they are placed on geomantic talismans. This is because the sigils used are traditional and not developed using a planetary magical square. Once again, here is an example of the difference between calling power from the earth and drawing power down from above.

Table 20
Sigils of spirits on earth talismans.

Name of Spirit	Planet	Sigil
Bartzabel	Mars	
Kedemel	Venus	
Taphthartharath	Mercury	
Chasmodai	Moon	
Sorath	Sun	
Zazel	Saturn	
Hismael	Jupiter	

Constructing an Earth Talisman

If they are made out of the usual paper or cardboard, earth talismans have much in common with the simple talismans described at the beginning of this chapter. Since they are simply depictions of the material world, they do not need to be divided into four levels of creation.

Earth talismans are usually circular or, less commonly, ten-sided decagons, with a single border. Within the border is written the divine name of Malkuth Adonai ha Aretz אדני הארז and Sandalphon שׂנדלפש, the archangel of Earth. An appropriate Bible verse can also be placed in this ring, if desired. A small, equal-armed cross, which acts as a full stop between the Hebrew letters, separates the names and the Bible verse.

In the talisman's heart is a nine-chambered square. In the central square is a sigil indicating the person for whom the talisman is being made. Arranged evenly about the personal sigil are seven of the geomantic figures representing the appropriate planet. Sometimes it will not be possible to fit all the figures within the eight spaces, and other times you will not find enough figures to fill that many spaces. There is no problem having empty boxes, and those times when there are too many geomantic figures, you should use your own intuition to select the ones you want on your talisman.

Above the grid, you should place the sigil or the name of the spirit of the planet. Below the grid, you should put your intention, preferably in a script like Celestial or Passing the River.

On the talisman's underside, the grid of geomantic figures and the person's sigil are repeated instead of the cross. This is because, unlike with planetary talismans, we want to connect the talisman to the earth powers mediated through the geomantic figures.

Figure 58 is an example of an earth talisman designed to protect someone called John Smith from physical attack. You can see a sigil designed by merging the letters *J* and *S* in the center of the grid. The sigil used is for the spirit Bartzabel, and the geomantic figures are derived from Puer and Rubeus.

Other Methods of Making Earth Talismans

For those of you who like getting your hands dirty, it is possible to make an earth talisman out of the real stuff. Take a flowerpot or wooden box, about a foot square and eight inches deep, and line the bottom of it with small, smooth stones.[7] Then place about six inches of good quality earth over the top.

Figure 58. An earth talisman designed to protect
someone from attack.

At an appropriate time and on an appropriate day of the week, thoroughly
dampen the earth with consecrated water.[8] Take a wooden stick or wand and draw
the talisman in the earth.[9] Carefully perform your consecration ritual and leave the
box outside for seven days. The box should be partly buried within the earth. The
earth should be covered if it rains and checked daily to see if the sigils have been
damaged. Any damage to the sigils' names and circle should be restored right away.
On each day that you tend to the talisman, you should try to visualize the earth
around the box turning into the appropriate planetary color.

After seven days, the earth and stones are to be buried. Visualize the correct planetary color tinting the earth and stones around the box. See this color seep into the
fiery center of the earth, taking with it your intention. Then see the energy flow up-
ward again so that every tree, shrub, and breath of wind seems to whisper your intention. The ground from your buried talisman has become sacred to that energy
and will work on the material plane to make sure your intention comes about.

Summary

You have completed the body of your talisman. Like the rabbis of old, you have
made your golem out of clay. For some talisman makers, the work stops here; they
believe that, having made the object, it is ready to do their bidding. You can see their

handiwork in many occult shops. While it may be pretty, your talisman is an inert piece of matter—now is the time to give your talisman its life breath. This is done using one of the magical rituals described in the next chapter.

1. The fact that we are not has to do with the cosmic issue of free will; in other words, we choose not to do so.

2. This was part of the additional side lecture for Golden Dawn students and was titled "Polygons and Polygrams." See Israel Regardie, ed., *The Golden Dawn,* 6th edition (Saint Paul, MN: Llewellyn Publishing, 1990) 505.

3. These were blind tests using the pendulum meters described in chapter 10.

4. I use John R. Kohlenberger's *Interlinear NIV Hebrew-English Old Testament* (Grand Rapids, MI: Zondervan, 1987). It is ideal for talisman makers who wish to use Hebrew notarikon Bible verses on their talismans.

5. I am aware that this is a generalization of the Seal of Truth's function, but a more complete explanation would fill a complete book.

6. There are some magicians who disagree with me on this point. They argue that the presence of geomantic symbols on talismans helps ground the force, enabling them to work on the material plane Assiah.

7. You might like to make a geomancy box as described by Chic and Sandra Tabatha Cicero in their book *Self-Initiation into the Golden Dawn Tradition* (Saint Paul, MN: Llewellyn Publishing, 1998).

8. This can be done by reciting the Banishing Ritual of the Pentagram in the appendix, but drawing the pentagrams on the surface of the water. Instead of saying "about me flame the pentagrams," say "the purifying pentagrams flame within the waters of the wise."

9. Do not use any metal objects.

9

Consecrating Talismans

Like Dr. Frankenstein, you have created an object that has all the potential to be alive. What is needed is a lightning bolt of divine energy that can jolt every cell into life. To do this we are going to use ritual.

Ritual is a talismanic act that draws occult power into the consciousness of the magician where it can be utilized. Magicians take symbols in a dramatic form to impress their microcosmic personal unconsciousness so that they can tap into macrocosmic powers. What a ritual to consecrate a talisman should do is to create the right conditions for that lightning bolt of divine energy to bring an ostensibly dead object to life.

In this chapter, we will look at three different rituals that utilize symbols and techniques that we have already examined. The first ritual is a simple, almost Shamanic consecration ceremony that uses chant and visualization to achieve its goal. The second ritual is a modern magical-lodge working, and the last ritual is a variation of the formula used by the adepts of the Esoteric Order of the Golden Dawn.

Creating Sacred Space

All ritual is conducted in space that is set aside and made special. What defines sacred space and makes it special is the mind of the magician. Rituals can be silently performed in the busiest of places if the magician has the ability to zone off part of his or her mind from intrusion, which takes practice. Occult students are trained in different techniques to do this.

The simplest technique is the "preparation of place" exercise that was taught by one of Dion Fortune's pupils, W. E. Butler.

Sit in a chair and relax as deeply as possible. Regularize your breathing so that your in-breaths take the same amount of time as your out-breaths.

Visualize yourself surrounded by a shell of impermeable, bright, blue light. Then meditate on the intention of your ritual.

Stray thoughts will appear in your mind, and the sounds of the outside world will distract you. As they appear, see them as objects, like birds or dogs, and gently push them outside the blue sphere.

Keep doing this until the space within the blue sphere is totally calm and quiet. Visualize a still candle of divine light in your heart—this represents your divine self.

Now visualize the blue sphere getting bigger until it fills the physical space in which you wish to work your ritual. As the blue light expands, it pushes aside all thought forms, people, and objects out of its way.

Now see the light of the candle glow brightly, filling your sacred space with divine presence and making the ground on which you stand holy.

It takes time to master this technique, but, once achieved, it is possible to work a ritual anywhere in the sort of calm that would only be achieved by a magician working in an isolated temple.

The Banishing Ritual of the Pentagram, which is given in the appendix, further purifies sacred space.

For the consecration of a talisman, a physical space free from intrusion is required. This can be a room, which is normally used for another purpose, that has been specially cleaned and "made sacred" by the preparation-of-space exercise and a Banishing Ritual of the Pentagram.

Equipment

Most rituals require some equipment. These are symbols that are important for giving life to your talisman. Meditation on each of these pieces of equipment will reveal much about the way the universe works. The most important symbol is the altar, on which is placed a candle that represents the divine presence and the talisman. In an ideal world the altar would be a double cube and be covered in a cloth of a color appropriate to the type of planetary force being used in your talisman; however, a covered table will do.

Consecrating Fire

The next piece of vital equipment is incense. Some people like to use commercially bought stick incense, but I don't feel that it generates enough smoke, nor does it have the same impressive qualities as incense placed on a burning charcoal. There are two schools of thought about the amount of smoke that is required for a ritual. Some people believe that a small amount, just enough to smell, is enough. Other people, myself included, believe that there should be enough smoke to create an impenetrable fog.[1] This enhances the magical atmosphere and provides a film screen for visualization.

Frankincense is a good general-purpose incense to use for consecration; however, if you want to add more power to your working you may want to mix it with one of the herbs or resins that are attributed to the appropriate planet. These will open centers in the brain that correspond to the various planetary forces.

Table 21
Planetary incense.

Planet	Herb, Wood, or Resin
Saturn	Cumin, pine, yew, myrrh, and sandalwood.
Jupiter	Nutmeg, ash, cedar, basil, and sage.
Mars	Tabacco, lignium aloes, rowan oil, and dragon's blood.
Sun	Frankencense, saffron, citrus fruit rind, mastic, and storax.
Venus	Rose, musk, jasmine, and violet.
Mercury	Cinnamon, cloves, galbanum, mace, and storax.
Moon	Myrtle, camphor, and myrrh.

Placing incense on a burning coal is a form of sacrifice and is one of the reasons modern magicians no longer kill wildlife in their rituals. The energy given off by the act of sacrifice of incense along with the power of the smell more than compensates for any power that is released by the death of an unfortunate animal.

A magician should acknowledge the sacrifice of the incense by saying:

Creature of Fire, by your sacrifice may all creatures seen and unseen be transformed to the image of that which formed the ages. Like a pillar of fire, you shall lead us, O Adonai.

Holy Water

The next vital component is "holy water." Earlier, I described how water may be consecrated using the Lesser Banishing Ritual of the Pentagram. Here is another technique.

Take a cup or bowl of water that is clear and free from physical impurities. Draw a banishing pentagram on the surface, saying:

Creature of Water, I exorcise thee and cleanse thee for my purpose.

Hold the water to your face so that you can see yourself reflected upon it.

May you be a reflection of the Ancient of Days, who moved upon the face of the waters and created all with an ineffable name.

Vibrate the name Yod, He, Vau, He, slowly. As you do so, visualize each letter in bright white in the center of the water. See the water glow with radiant energy.

The Triangle of the Art

The magician's *triangle of the art* is a magical drawing that is so powerful that it can be used to bring spirits and angels into physical manifestation. The manufacture of talismans does not require the spirits and angels to appear physically before us, but a triangle of the art does assist them in moving down the levels of creation to impregnate the talisman with their energy.

In chapter 8, the triangle was attributed to Binah and Saturn (figure 40). According to the Cabbalists, Binah is the womb of creation, and from within it all things came forth. The Saturnian influence also helps to keep any force within the triangle. Around the perimeters of the triangle are the Greek names of power Tetragrammatron, Primematum, and Anexhexeton, and inside the triangle is the name of the archangel Michael (figure 59).

Figure 59. The triangle of the art.

Michael is the warrior of God, and it is his job keep control of demonic and other unbalanced forces. This applies to the energies we are calling to impregnate our talisman. Although they are not demonic, they do have their bad sides and Michael's energy helps keep them in check.

A triangle of the art works like a lift shaft to the heavens, or a teleportation pad in a *Star Trek* episode. The angel and spirit's energies will be focused within the triangle and will not escape. It is unsafe for a magician to enter the triangle because he or she would be unable to handle the concentrated power levels within its borders. A talisman is placed within the triangle, where it receives the full force of angelic power. The magician, like someone handling nuclear material, only touches the talisman with a magic wand.

In talisman consecrations, a triangle of the art can be painted on cardboard and placed on the altar. Alternatively, its outline and its names of protection can be drawn in the imagination using a wand.

On each corner of the triangle of the art, you should place a candle that is the color of the planetary force called. Ideally, there should be three incense burners placed alongside the candles, but these are optional in this type of working.

After the temple has been purified, trace the triangle's outline with the wand while vibrating the divine names that are written on the triangle's borders. Vibrating the name Michael, visualize the archangel standing in the triangle. Then light the candles and incense burners before proceeding with the ritual.

Once the ritual is completed, purify and consecrate the triangle, and then say:

> *In the name of Tetragrammatron, Primematum, and Anexhexeton, I declare this triangle of the art closed.*

Then, with a wand, draw an equal-armed cross in the center of the triangle. Trace the triangle's outline again, imagining the lines unwinding like string and entering into the wand.

The Cabbalistic Shamanic Approach to Consecrating a Talisman

Shaman-type consecrations use more primitive magical techniques at the expense of elaborate rituals. This does not make them less effective, but it does put a different sort of pressure on the magician.

Research into Shamanic techniques indicates that there are similar techniques in use throughout the world. Most involve chanting and vision quests into the underworld. These techniques have influenced religion and magic for thousands of years.

Mystical Cabbalah fits in very well with some aspects of Shamanism. Cabbalists often chanted divine or angelic names to send themselves into a trancelike state, where there were granted visions and knowledge. The founder of the Chassidic movement, Baal Shem Tov, took this one step further and added dance and music to help send Cabbalists into ecstatic visions.

By taking these Cabbalistic developments and incorporating some of the more Shamanic techniques, we have a powerful method of consecrating our talismans.

Preparation

The talisman should be made and a journey taken to the planetary temple to meet with the beings whose names are to be placed on the talisman. After their consent has been given, the talisman should be placed on an appropriate flashing tablet until charged.

Before the ritual, the preparation-of-place exercise should be performed as well as a Banishing Ritual of the Pentagram.

Equipment

Clothing should be as loose as possible. In the center of the room should be an altar or a table. There should be enough space in the room for the magician to walk a circle without having to step over any furniture.

A flashing magical square should be placed on the altar with an unlit candle beside it.

In the South of the altar is an incense burner, and in the West is the consecrated water. In the East is a wand or staff, and in the North is a pot of earth.

The Rite

Stand in the North, facing the South and holding the talisman. Lighting the candle, say:

The light shines in the darkness and the shadows flee.

Walk to the East, take the staff, salute with it, and say:

I send my voice beyond the East to the gates of the Dawn. Come forth, mighty Raphael, and be welcome in this circle.

Putting down the staff, walk to the South, pick up the incense burner, and salute the South with it:

I send my voice beyond the South to the gates of the Noon. Come forth, mighty Michael, and be welcome in this circle.

Putting down the burner, walk to the West, pick up the holy water, and salute the West with it:

I send my voice beyond the West to the gates of the Setting Sun. Come forth, mighty Gabriel, and be welcome in this circle.

Putting down the water, walk to the North, pick up the earth, and salute the North with it:

I send my voice beyond the North to the gates of the Midnight. Come forth, mighty Uriel, and be welcome in this circle.

Complete the circle and carefully visualize each of the four archangels surrounding the circle. Then go the South and face East. Visualize the altar turning into a huge tree. See the tree put down roots deep into the soil and its branches reaching into the heavens. The candle and magic tablet are nestling in a hollow.

Take the talisman to the South and pass it through the smoke. Visualize it burning with white fire and re-forming until it returns to its proper shape.

Then take the talisman to the North and touch each corner with consecrated water. Visualize the water permeating every part of the talisman and purifying it. Talking to the talisman, say:

Creature of talismans, by water and by fire thou art purified and consecrated for my purpose.

Go to the West and face the tree. Looking up into the heavens, say:

I call into the heavens to the mighty name (insert the appropriate one). If it be thy will, bless this talisman with life so that it may (read the talisman's intention). Do this as I chant thy holy name.

Taking the talisman in your hand, walk clockwise around the circle, slowly chanting the appropriate divine name. You must keep your pace even and steady and resist any temptation to speed up the chanting. Meditate as you chant the divine name and the talisman's intention. There is no limit to the number of times you chant the name or the number of times you complete the circle. After a while, you will start to feel lightheaded, even a little dizzy. Always focus on the divine name and seek to contact it. After a while, you will sense a divine presence, or the tree in the center of the room will start to glow white, or you will achieve a state of bliss. Whatever happens, you will know when the contact has been made. When this happens, place the talisman on the magic square. Visualize the divine energy pouring down the tree and through your heart into the talisman. Watch the letters of the divine-name portion of the talisman light up. Say:

Praise be to (insert the divine name) who has blessed this talisman with divine purpose.

Then, return to the West, look up, and say:

> *I call into the heavens to the mighty archangel (insert the appropriate one). If it be*
> *thy will, bless this talisman with life so that it may (read the talisman's intention).*
> *Do this as I chant thy name.*

Now repeat your circle-walking, holding the talisman and chanting the name of the archangel. Once again you will need to rely on your intuition to know when to stop. Place the talisman on the magic square and visualize the power descending. This time, as the power flows through you and the tree, carefully outline the sigil of the archangel above the talisman over the correct position of the letters of the magic square. You should visualize the sigil hanging in the air above the talisman. When the talisman is taken off the magic square, visualize the sigil orbiting around the talisman about eight inches away.

Repeat the chanting and sealing process for the angel of the planet. Then, standing over the talisman, draw the sigil of the spirit of the planet and say:

> *In the name (divine name) and by the order of (archangel and angel), I com-*
> *mand the spirit (say the name of the spirit and draw the sigil in the air above the*
> *magic square) to work through this creature of talismans to (read the talisman's*
> *intention).*

Finally, consecrate and purify the talisman with fire and water again. Then say:

> *Creature of talismans, agent of the power of (insert planetary name), I set thee to*
> *thy work in the name of (insert divine name). Let it be so!*

Meditate for a while on the work you have done before standing before the tree. Vibrate the word AGLA and visualize the tree shrinking and returning to the shape of your altar. Say:

> *The rite is done. May all creatures seen and unseen who have assisted in this*
> *working depart to their own kingdoms in peace. And may those creatures who*
> *may have been accidentally caught within the web of my magic be free to go in*
> *peace. May the blessing of the Crown of Crowns descend upon you all.*

Go to each quarter, starting at the East and finishing in the North, and say:

Peace in this quarter let the doors of the Sun be closed.

Then perform a Cabbalistic Cross and a Banishing Ritual of the Pentagram.

Modern Talisman Lodge Working

Magical rituals have become more simplified and less scripted in recent years (some say at the expense of good technique). Below is scripted a consecration rite for one person using what I call the Dion Fortune tradition or post–Golden Dawn British magic. It is more structured than the Shamanic working, but easier to perform than the Golden Dawn–style ritual.

It uses a technique that was developed in the Golden Dawn called *god-form assumption*. It is a simple technique, but should be practiced beforehand.

To assume a god-form (in this case an archangel and an angel), visualize a small statue of the being between your feet.

Imagine a star high above your head and see a silver thread touch the top of your head, go down your spine, and connect with the statue. The statue comes alive and grows within you until it is slightly below the level of your eyes. Never allow the image to get bigger.

Now allow part of your consciousness to enter into mind-to-mind contact with the being. During this time you will feel part-human, part-deity, but you should not allow the god-form to take control.

Perform any work that you need to and don't be too surprised if your voice changes when you do it. There are a number of times where I have seen deep-voiced, male magicians suddenly speak with a woman's voice when assuming a god-form and, becoming so shocked, they have lost contact with the being.

When the work is finished, allow the god-form to shrink to the size of the statue and allow the light from the star to disconnect and retract. You should always perform a Cabbalistic Cross after god-form work.

Preparing the Lodge Room

In the lodge room, there should be a candle placed in each quarter and an altar in the center. A night-light in a blue bowl is placed in the East to represent the divine presence. In the center on the altar is the triangle of the art, the appropriate magic square, and the three candles.

In the East in front of the blue light, is a chair with a magic wand or staff. In the South is an incense burner (and a sword if you have one); in the West, an empty chalice; and in the North, a dish of bread and salt. You should wear a black or white robe.

Preparation

As with the Shamanic working, a journey should be taken to the planetary temple to meet with the appropriate beings to get their consent for its use. The talisman should be placed on an appropriate flashing tablet until charged.

Again, the preparation-of-place exercise should be performed before the Banishing Ritual of the Pentagram. Then walk around the perimeter of the temple in a wide circle holding the light of the presence. While doing so, imagine that the candle is leaving a line of light in its wake. Once the circle is complete, walk a line from the East to the altar, from the South to the altar, from the West to the altar, and from the North to the altar. When finished, you will have drawn an equal-armed cross enclosed in a circle and defined the way that power will flow during the working. Place the lamp behind the chair in the East and then stand in the East.

Visualize yourself as a silver chalice. Looking to the heavens, visualize a star high in the heavens. Then see a silver light descend from the star and pour into yourself. This light should fill you up and overflow into the temple until the room is full of white mist. The incense should then be lit and the rite started.

The Rite

Go to the East and perform a Middle Pillar exercise. Then aspire to the highest concept of Deity that you can. When you feel full of the divine white brilliance, turn to the temple and say:

> *From those who see the light of the most high face unto face, I bring you greetings!*

There is a pause and then say:

> *Let this lodge of the mysteries be opened in the ancient manner.*

Walk to the East, salute, and say:

> *O thou whose name is Limitless*
> *O thou whose name is Greatness and Peace*
> *O thou who bears us on the path of the dawn*[2]
> *Thee I adore and Thee I invoke. May my life be a everlasting and continual sacrifice unto thee.*

Now, in your mind's eye, journey to the planetary temple appropriate to the talisman that you are making. Visualize this temple as being within your current physical lodge. Take your time over this and try and make it appear as real as possible. Then go to the East and perform a Cabbalistic Cross, draw an invoking earth pentagram, and say:

> *I open the portal of the East in the sacred name (insert the divine name of the Cabbalistic sphere attributed to the planet).*

Visualize a gate opening onto a sky scene with a gentle wind blowing, and then go South. Repeat the opening phrase, but when the door opens, visualize yourself looking out on a fiery volcanic landscape. Go to the West and repeat the opening phrase. This time visualize a seascape with a full moon rising. Finally, go to the North, repeat the opening phrase, and visualize a lamp in a cave. Return to the East and say:

> *Before me, Raphael, behind me, Gabriel, on my right hand, Michael, on my left hand, Uriel, I am upheld by Sandalphon and strive for Metatron, and within me dwells the hidden one.*

Perform a Cabbalistic Cross and then go the West of the altar and face East. Place your palms together and place them above the altar. Then, as you say the following, separate your hands as if you were opening a curtain.

> *In the name of (insert the divine name) and through the power channeled through me in earth, I declare this temple OPEN to the beckoning light.*

Visualize light flooding into the temple from this gateway that you have just opened. Take the incense and cense the altar three times. Then take the water from the West and circle the altar, scattering holy water and saying:

Heaven's holy waters descend on this place as a blessing and purification.

Then light the quarter candles in the East, saying:

Behold Raphael clothed in the Dawn. Come and favor me with thy presence.

Visualize Raphael arriving and then move to the South, light the candle, and say:

Behold Michael clothed in the flames of the Holy One. Come, glorious Michael, and favor me with thy presence.

Repeat the process in the West, saying:

Behold Gabriel clothed in the Heavenly Dew. Come, mighty Gabriel, and favor me with thy presence.

Repeat the process in the North, saying:

Behold Uriel clothed with the crystals and fruits of earth and crowned with lightning. Come, powerful Uriel, and favor us with thy presence.

Return to the West, face East, and say:

Holy art thou, Lord of the Universe
Holy art thou whom nature hath not formed
Holy art thou the vast and the mighty one
Lord of the Light and of the Darkness.
Thee we adore and we thee invoke.

Pause and say:

The intention of this working, if it please the divine, is to create a talisman of (insert planet) to (read the intention of the talisman). So mote it be!

Open the triangle of the art. Then raise your wand above the talisman.

O thou who art (insert divine name), God made manifest in the sphere of (name the sphere on the Tree of Life), bless and empower this talisman to (read intention).

Chant the divine name once and visualize a shaft of white light descending on the triangle. Chant it again and see the letters start to glow with white light. Chant it a third time and see the outer ring of the talisman light up. Then read the Bible verse, if you have used one, and see these letters light up as you speak.

Go East, face East, and say:

In the name of (insert divine name), I ask (insert the name of the archangel of the sphere on the Tree of Life) to assist me.

Assume the god-form of the archangel of the sphere. When you are ready, raise the wand and vibrate the name of the archangel:

By the power of my name, I seal and awaken this talisman.

Then vibrate the name of the archangel of the planet and draw its sigil above the talisman.

By the power of (insert archangel of the planet), I seal and awaken this talisman.

See the archangel of the planet hover briefly in the triangle of the art. See its name on the talisman light up and the sigil hover around it. Then vibrate the name of the intelligence of the planet and draw its sigil above the talisman.

By the power of (insert the name of the intelligence of the planet), I seal and awaken this talisman.

Visualize the intelligence of the planet hovering briefly in the triangle of the art. See its name on the talisman light up and the sigil hover around it. Then vibrate the name of the spirit of the planet and draw its sigil above the talisman.

By the power of (insert the name of the spirit of the planet), I seal and awaken this talisman.

Visualize the intelligence of the planet hovering briefly in the triangle of the art. See its name on the talisman light up and the sigil hover around it.

Pointing the wand at the talisman see the divine light behind you in the East. Allow it to flow into you, into the archangel, down the wand, and into the talisman.

In the name of (insert divine name) and under the authority of (insert archangel),
may (intelligence and spirit) work through this talisman to (insert intention). In
the name of (insert divine name), let the light be extended and this talisman live!
So mote it be.

Visualize the planetary seal on the talisman bursting into life followed by the whole talisman in a firework of appropriate colors. Purify it, consecrate it, and unseal the triangle of the art. Meditate briefly on the work you have done. Then, raising your hands, say:

Thanks to thee, O Lord of the Universe, for thy help this day.

Pause for a moment and then say:

Let this temple be closed in the Ancient manner.

Go to the East, draw a Banishing Pentagram of Earth, and then say:

I close the portal of the East in the sacred name of (insert the divine name of the
planet).

Visualize the gate closing so that the wall appears. Then go to the South. Draw the Pentagram and repeat the closing phrase. Repeat this in the West and then in the North. Return to the East and say:

Around me protect the pentagrams, above me are the archangels of God, and
within me dwells the hidden one.

Perform a Cabbalistic Cross and then go to the West of the altar and face East. Draw your hands together as if you were closing a curtain.

In the name of (insert the divine name) and through the power channeled
through me in earth, I declare this temple closed.

Allow the visualization of the planetary temple to melt away and be replaced by the earth-plane temple. Then perform a Banishing Ritual of the Pentagram.

The Golden Dawn Empowerment Ritual

The Golden Dawn ritual is considerably more involved than the other two consecration rituals. It is based on the first ritual that Golden Dawn candidates undergo—that of the 0 = 0 ritual. This ritual was designed to take the candidates out of the darkness of ignorance and introduce them to their higher selves. This experience started the process of freeing the divine aspects of individuals from the constraints of matter—literally making that which appeared dead come to life.

It is not surprising that this ritual makes a good basis for bringing an inanimate object, like a drawing on a piece of cardboard, into a new life as a planetary talisman.

When Golden Dawn candidates passed the relevant examinations, they were taught the hidden formula of the 0 = 0 ritual, which they used to construct their own rituals. These rituals were designed to take the 0 = 0 formula and adapt it so that one person could work it alone. Israel Regardie published one such ritual for the consecration of a Jupiter talisman in his Golden Dawn book. I have worked this ritual with some success, but feel it is time that it was updated.

In order to do this, I have looked at the original formula, called Z1, which decreed what actions should happen at key points in the ritual.

Since the magician will not have any officers for this working, he or she will have to say some of the officer's phrases or new statements in their place. One of the founders of the Golden Dawn, MacGregor Mathers, wrote an additional formula called the Z2 documents, which proscribed steps for the consecration of a talisman.

There are those who believe that inner-order Golden Dawn work has to follow religiously those seven rituals written by Israel Regardie. They believe that these were specific rituals that came from the official vaults of the Golden Dawn and must only be adapted to suit the different intentions of their workings. No one qualified in the Esoteric Order of the Golden Dawn, or the lodges who follow Regardie's instructions, believes this.

Regardie wrote the seven rituals as guidelines for others to use—they were not used by the Golden Dawn. Other Golden Dawn magicians had rituals of their own; indeed, they were required to write them as part of their coursework. I have seen some original Golden Dawn rituals, which on the surface look so different that if you did not have Z2 manuscripts to follow, you would not recognize them as Golden Dawn workings.

This book is not the place to break down the mechanics of the Golden Dawn system of magic. Pat Zalewski[3] and Chic and Sandra Tabatha Cicero[4] have performed that task more expertly than I could in their books. This rite, although written using Mather's guidelines, is devised for those who have not been initiated into the Golden Dawn tradition and is stripped of some of the equipment used by the Order's practitioners. Those who are members of the Golden Dawn can easily place all the relevant equipment into the working. Those with knowledge of the Z2 documents will be aware that I have left out several of the procedures after the talisman's consecration. This is because I have not found them to make much difference to the consecration process. They were influenced heavily by Mathers' enthusiasm for the theater of the Key of Solomon system rather than any practical magical requirement.

Equipment You Will Need

You wil need a white or black robe with red socks. You will also need a wand, a lantern, an altar, an incense burner with appropriate incense, a glass of consecrated water, two large candles on individual stands (one black and the other white) or black and white pillars,[5] a triangle of the art with three appropriately colored candles at each angle, an appropriate flashing magic square, a black bag and a black cord or ribbon, and a banner of the East and West.[6]

Before the Ritual

Construct your talisman and leave it on an appropriate flashing tablet until it is charged. Set up the temple according to figure 60 on an appropriate day and at an appropriate time. Place the talisman in the corner of the room beside the lamp.

Light the candles and the incense. Holding your wand, stand in the East beside the banner of the East. Place the talisman by the lamp. Visualize yourself in an Egyptian temple. Behind you on a throne is the Egyptian god Osirus; in front of you between the pillars is the goddess Maat; and beside the banner of the West is the god Horus. By the lamp is the jackal-headed Anubus; by the incense burner is the goddess Thaum Aesch Niaeth;[7] and by the water is the goddess Auramo-ooth.[8]

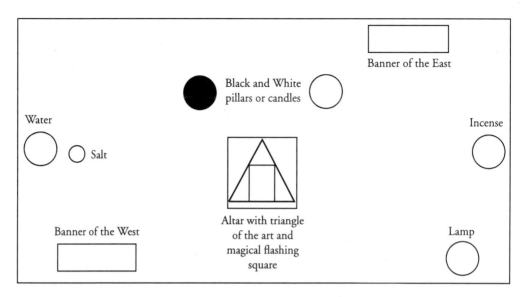

Figure 60. Golden Dawn temple plan.

Around the walls are beings dressed alike in kilts and nemyss of black and yellow. Some are human, but others are animals. Each wears a necklace in the shape of a flying hawk and carries a flail in the left hand. These are the forty-two assessors—the force of cosmic justice that judges all, including the gods.

The Rite

Perform a Banishing Ritual of the Pentagram, a Cabbalistic Cross, and a Middle Pillar exercise.

Visualize yourself as Osirus. Raise your wand and point at the talisman on the other side of the temple. Stamp your foot and, as you do so, allow a current of energy to pass from your heart center toward the talisman. See the talisman start to vibrate.

Walk to the lantern and pick it up in your left hand. Visualize yourself as Anubis. Walk to the Northwest, raise your wand on high, extend the lantern so that the light floods the temple, and say:

Hekas, Hekas Este Bebaloi.

Return the lantern to its place. Return to the South via the East and become Thaum Aesch Niaeth. Take the incense burner and work clockwise around the temple, saying:

When, after all the phantoms have vanished, thou shalt see that holy and formless fire, that fire which darts and flashes through the hidden depths of the Universe, hear thou the Voice of Fire.

After reaching the South, become Thaum Aesch Niaeth. Shake some incense three times before the wall. Make a large circle, tracing the Invoking Pentagram of Fire within it,[9] then draw the sign of Leo in the center, saying:

In the name of Elohim Gibor, I invoke ye, ye Angels of the Watchtower of the South.

Go to the North[10] and become Auramo-ooth. Pick up then glass of water, sprinkle a few drops of water, and circumambulate clockwise, saying:

So therefore first, the priest who governeth the works of fire must sprinkle with the lustral water of the loud resounding sea.

Go to the West, sprinkle water three and with cup make circle, with the Invoking Water Pentagram within it, then Eagle Kerub in the center, vibrating:

Shaddai El Chai. I invoke ye, ye Angels of the Watchtower of the West.

Return to the West. Become Aroueris,[11] shake the wand three times, then circumambulate, saying:

Such a fire existeth, extending through the rushing of Air. Or even a fire formless, whence cometh the image of a voice. Or even a flashing light, abounding, revolving, whirling forth, crying aloud.

On returning to the East, strike Air three times with the wand; then make circle, with Invoking Air Pentagram within it, with sign of Aquarius for Air in center, saying:

Yod Heh Vav Heh Aloah Ve Daath, I invoke ye, ye Angels of the Watchtower of the East.

Go to the West and become Horus. Go to the North and pick up the salt. Sprinkle the salt and circumambulate, saying:

Stoop not down into that darkly splendid world wherein continually lieth a faithless depth and Hades wrapped in gloom, delighting in unintelligible images, precipitous, winding; a black ever-rolling abyss, ever espousing a body unluminous, formless, and void.

On returning to the North, sprinkle more salt, then make a circle with the Invoking Earth Pentagram within it, with Sign of Taurus for Earth Kerub in center, saying:

Adonai Ha Aretz, I invoke ye, ye Angels of the Watchtower of the North.

Stand between the pillars, facing the altar. Use the wand to describe Invoking Pentagrams of Spirit (within circle), both active and passive, vibrate:

Yeheshuah, I invoke ye, ye divine forces of the Spirit of Life.

Make the Sign of the Rending of the Veil. (Stretch your hands before you, then separate them sharply, as if opening a curtain.) Then say:

I invoke ye, ye Angels of the celestial spheres, whose dwelling is in the invisible. Ye are the guardians of the gates of the Universe, be ye also the guardians of this mystic sphere. Keep far removed the evil and the unbalanced. Strengthen and inspire me so that I may preserve unsullied this abode of the mysteries of the eternal Gods. Let my sphere be pure and holy so that I may enter in and become a partaker of the secrets of the Light Divine.

Pause and then go East and assume Aroueris.

Let the darkness be rolled asunder, let the Mystical Circumambulation in the path of light begin.

Circumambulate three times clockwise, beginning at the East. Make the sign of the Enterer followed by the sign of silence each time you pass the East.

Return to the West of the altar and utter the Adoration as yourself. Make the sign of the enterer at the end of the first three lines; each time you must strive to make a connection to the divine light. Make the sign of silence at the end of the fourth line, right arm hanging by your side. Raise the index and third fingers of your left hand to your lips.

> *Holy art thou, Lord of the Universe.*
> *Holy art thou, whom Nature hath not formed.*
> *Holy art thou, the Vast and the Mighty One.*
> *Lord of the Light and the Darkness.*

Go to the East, become Aroueris, and say:

> *The purpose of this working, if it please the Divine, is to bring a talisman of (insert appropriate planet) to life.*

Go to the West and become Anubis. Place the talisman in the bag and tie it with a ribbon. Make sure that it is possible to expose part of the talisman to the light when required. Go between the pillars and become Maat:

> *Creature of talismans, arise and enter the darkness.*

Go to the West, become Anubis, and tell the talisman:

> *Unconsecrated and unpurified, you may not enter this hall.*

Go to the North and become Auramo-ooth. Go to the talisman (clockwise around the temple), place three drops of water on the black bag, and say:

> *I purify you with water.*

Go to the South and become Thaum Aesch Niaeth. Go to the talisman (clockwise around the temple), cense the black bag three times, and say:

> *I consecrate thee with fire.*

Place the talisman at the foot of the altar. Go to the East, become Osirus, and say:

> *Creature of talismans. It is the intention of this working that you shall become a living example of the planet (insert planet) and to work entirely to the goal of (insert intention).*

Become Anubis and place the talisman in the triangle of the art upon the flashing magic square. Activate the triangle.

Go East and become Aroueris. Become aware of your heart center. Breathe out and allow a rose pink energy to be projected outward so that it hovers at about the height of your head on your side of the pillars. With your will, shape it into a sphere. Say the following invocation and, as you state each name, draw the sigil in the sphere and see them both remain within the sphere.

> *O thou who art (insert divine name). If it be thy will, let the archangel (insert archangel of the planet) send forth a current so that (insert intelligence of the planet) shall order (insert spirit of the planet) to bring about (insert intention).*

Go to the West and become Horus. See in your hands a large sword of light. Go to the triangle of the art, place the imaginary sword on the talisman, and say:

> *Creature of talismans, thou art bound to your intention from which you may not deviate. In your work you may not transgress the will of the Divine.*

Go to the West and become Anubis. With your wand, carefully remove the talisman from the triangle of the art, and then leave it in the North. Go to the East, become Osirus, and say:

> *The Voice of my Undying Soul and Secret Soul said unto me, "Let me enter the Path of Darkness and peradventure, there shall find the Light. I am the only Being in the Abyss of Darkness; from an Abyss of Darkness came I forth ere my birth, from the Silence of a Primal Sleep." And the Voice of Ages said unto my Soul, "I am He who formulates in Darkness, the Light that shineth in Darkness, yet the Darkness comprehendeth it not."*

Return to the West and become Anubis. Taking the lamp go to the North. Pick up the talisman, and circumambulate to the South. Put the talisman down. Go to the North, become Auramo-ooth, and purify the talisman Return the water to the North and go to the South. Become Thaum Aesch Niaeth and consecrate the talisman. Go to the West, pick up the lantern, and say:

> *Creature of talismans, twice purified you may enter the path of the West.*

Take the talisman to the West. Put down the lamp, and slightly reveal the talisman. Become Horus. Point the imaginary sword of light at the talisman and say:

> *Thou canst not pass from concealment unto manifestation, save by virtue of the name Elohim. Before all things are the Chaos and the Darkness, and the gates of the land of Night. I am He whose Name is Darkness. I am the great One of the Paths of the Shades. I am the Exorcist in the midst of the Exorcism. Take on therefore manifestation without fear before me, for I am he in whom fear is Not. Thou hast known me.*

Become Anubis and replace the veil. Take the talisman to the North where you place it on the ground and purify and consecrate it again with water and fire as before. Become Anubis and say:

> *Creature of Talismans, thrice consecrate, thou mayest approach the Gate of the East.*

Go to the Northeast. Put the lantern and talisman down. Unveil the talisman partly, become Osirus, and say:

> *Thou canst not pass from concealment unto manifestation save by virtue of the name YHVH. After the formless and the Void and the Darkness, then cometh the knowledge of the Light. I am that Light which riseth in darkness. I am the Exorcist in the midst of the Exorcism. Take on therefore manifestation before me, for I am the wielder of the forces of the Balance. Thou hast known me now so pass thou on unto the Cubical Altar of the Universe.*

Become Anubis and cover the talisman again. Take it to the triangle of the art and push it onto the magic square with the wand.

Go between the pillars and become Maat. With the wand over the triangle of the art, say the following invocation. As you state each name, draw the sigil in the air. See an image of the angel called appear briefly in the triangle of the art about the talisman.

> *O thou who art (insert divine name). If it be thy will, let the archangel (insert archangel of the planet) send forth a current so that (insert intelligence of the planet) shall order (insert spirit of the planet) to bring about (insert intention).*

Pause. Carefully take the talisman out of the triangle of the art and unwrap it. Keep the cord tied around it. Then go to the East, become Aroueris, and say:

> *Creature of talismans, long you have lived in darkness. Quit the night and seek the day. Behold, your life's purpose comes upon you.*

Step slowly toward the pink sphere. Push it between the pillars and into the triangle of the art using the sign of the enterer as you say the following:

> *I come in the power of the light.*
> *I come in the light of wisdom.*
> *I come in the mercy of the light.*
> *The light hath healing in its wings.*

See the pink sphere and its sigils merge with those in the triangle of the art. Draw an Invoking Planetary Hexagram[12] in the triangle of the art with the wand, and say:

> *By the names, powers, and rites already rehearsed, I conjure upon thee power and might irresistible.*

Then say these mystical words:

> *Khabs Am Pekht, Knox om Pax, Light in Extension.*

Feel the divine current behind you. Open up your heart center to it, and propel it outward with the sign of the enterer into the talisman. Do so until you feel your willpower weakening, and then perform the sign of silence. The talisman should be glowing with power, and its letters should appear to be aflame. Close the triangle of the art. Go to the West and become Anubis. Take the cord from the talisman, and say:

> *By the name of (insert divine name), I invoke upon thee the power of (insert planetary name).*

Circumambulate three times holding the talisman in your right hand.

Now talk to the talisman, explaining what it is required to do, and wrap it or put it in a box.

Take the lantern, go to the Northeast, and say:

Hekas Hekas Este Bebaloi.
I now release any spirits that may have been imprisoned by this ceremony. Depart
in peace to your own habitations with the blessing of Yeheshuah.

Return the lantern and then, as yourself, allow the temple of Maat to fade. Perform the Banishing Ritual of the Hexagram and then the Banishing Ritual of the Pentagram. Then say:

I now declare this temple closed.

---

1. Some people can't handle this amount of smoke, while others belive too much is a distraction. However much smoke you use, it is vital to disconnect your fire alarm!

2. This is inspired by Utterance 569 of the Pyramid Texts. See R. O. Faulkner, *The Ancient Egyptian Pyramid Texts* (Oxford University Press, 1969) 22.

3. See Pat Zalewski, *Z-5: Secret Teachings of the Golden Dawn, Book 1: The Neophyte Ritual 0 = 0* (Saint Paul, MN: Llewellyn Publishing, 1991).

4. See Chic and Sandra Tabatha Cicero, *Self-Initiation into the Golden Dawn Tradition.* (Saint Paul, MN: Llewellyn Publishing, 1998) and *Creating Magical Tools* (Saint Paul, MN: Llewellyn Publishing, 1999).

5. See Chic and Sandra Tabatha Cicero, *Creating Magical Tools* (Saint Paul, MN: Llewellyn Publishing, 1999).

6. These are optional. For details on their construction, see Chic and Sandra Tabatha Cicero, *Secrets of a Golden Dawn Temple* (Saint Paul, MN: Llewellyn Publishing, 1992).

7. Thaum Aesch Niaeth looks like Isis and wears a vulture headdress and wears red.

8. Auramo-ooth also looks like Isis, only this time she wears blue.

9. See appendix.

10. This position differs from Israel Regardie's "Opening by Watchtower" ritual because it is based on the format of the outer order temple, which places the officers in different places. Even though the position of the North is attributed to Earth, the Officer responsible for purification and water, the Stolistes, is stationed in the North during the ritual. According to Z2, the Golden Dawn initiates were instructed to "prepare the circle" at this point and many use Regardie's watchtower ritual (which is based on an inner order ceremony); however, Z2 specifies that the outer order temple layout should be used.

11. Aroueris is a hawk-headed god of the Sun, like Ra.

12. See appendix.

10

Making Sure the Talisman Is Working

How do you know if the talisman you have made is working properly? For centuries, people only knew this when their talisman got the desired result. For example, a healing talisman was deemed to have worked properly if recovery resulted soon after its manufacture, and a travel talisman worked if the journey was successful. Unfortunately, for a lot of reasons, some talismans do not work. In this chapter, we are going to look at why they are faulty and how to fix them.

What Can Go Wrong?

Talisman making is a complicated magical act. There are a number of things that can go wrong in the manufacture of a talisman that can weaken it so badly that it is ineffectual.

The most obvious source of faults is the consecration ritual. Since this is where the talisman comes to life, a failure at this point is the most common reason why one doesn't work.

I know of one person who was making talismans commercially. After careful manufacture of about a dozen different talismans, he would perform a general consecration ceremony for all of them. This meant that the energy from the ritual was divided between twelve different talismans; and each talisman, while designed to receive planetary force, was only receiving a general charge. As a result, the talismans had an energy that a psychic could pick up, but it was not focused enough to do its required task properly.

Other ritual problems include sections of the rite being left out. This is surprisingly common as rituals are conducted in semidarkness and pages of text sometimes go astray. In one ritual, I saw that a vital consecration and purification was left out, and the talisman couldn't attract enough divine energy needed for it to burst into life. Another time, an invocation to an archangel was left out, which weakened the talisman so badly that it was rendered useless.

Failure may also result if the magician has a problem with a particular energy. It is impossible for you to invoke energy successfully if you have a conscious or subconscious block against that energy. Someone who has a fear of death will have a problem invoking Saturn; someone who has a problem with men might have difficulty with solar talismans, and somone who has a problem with women might have a problem with Moon talismans. A person who can't communicate will not be able to make a Mercury talisman, and someone who has no love or creativity will find it impossible to make a Venus talisman.

One way of discovering what blocks you might have would be to consult your astrological chart. If you have oppositions and squares to any of the planets, it is possible that you will have difficulty dealing with those particular energies. For example, someone whose Sun is opposed to his or her Moon or whose planets are badly placed could have problems manifesting these forces in a talisman.

Sometimes these problems will prevent people from making talismans until these energies are properly integrated in their lives. Someone with the Sun opposing the Moon might have to resolve the psychological damage caused by warring parents, while another might have to get in touch with his or her emotions before making a Venus talisman.

In some circumstances, you will have difficulty making a talisman for yourself. If you want something too badly, your lack of that object could lead to an obsession. Rather than drawing that object closer to you, an obsession only reinforces the lack and pushes the object further away. When you come to make and consecrate a talisman, that obsession is worked into the talisman's aura and helps to make the object even less obtainable. This is particularly true of "love" talismans that are focused on a particular individual for whom the magician has an attraction.

For this reason, some talismans are best made by other people who are not connected to your intention; however, bear in mind that a wise magician would make a talisman to cure the obsession first.

One friend of mine was obsessed with a woman who alternated between leading him on and rejecting him. Something in the woman's behavior triggered something within the man's psyche until he could think of nothing but her. He was so desperate for this woman to be his totally that he ignored her personality and allowed her to treat him very badly. Finally, after yet another moment of rejection, he approached a fellow magician for help. The obsession had left him battered and drained and he finally turned to magic to bring the woman to him.

The magician suggested that it would be unethical to make a talisman that would bend the woman to the man's will, but that he could make one that would heal the relationship. The man believed that the relationship would only be healed if the woman were in his arms. What actually happened was that the woman got bored with her game with my friend and found another man. She designed her new game so that she could be hostile and humiliate my friend, remaining in contact so that the game could continue. After two weeks of refusing to see the obsessed man and being quite vile in her dealings with him, he started to wake up to what she was really like.

The woman he was dealing with was so unlike the image he had of her. Confused, he went into counseling. It only took a few sessions before the man realized the psychological roots of the obsession and lost interest in the woman completely. He gained in self-confidence and is now involved in a balanced and loving relationship. In this case, a dysfunctional relationship was "cured" by its termination.

Talismans to "obtain" a particular loved one were the stock and trade of charlatans for millennia. They are possible to make (but not by using any of the entities in this book); however, they result in someone being bound to a person against his or her will. This does not quench the need for love, it just fuels an obsession. Generally, it is better to make a talisman that will help make someone more loveable and self-confident. In other words, cure the cause of the lack of love rather than the symptom.

How can weak points in a magician's character be overcome temporarily to the point that he or she can make a talisman? Obsessions aside, this can be achieved over a period of time, before the consecration ceremony. Once the talisman has been constructed and placed on the flashing tablet, you should sit before it in meditation every day. Perform a Middle Pillar exercise followed by the full Tree of Life exercise given in chapter 3.

Once the Tree is lit up in your aura, focus on the sphere on the Tree of Life that is relevant to the talisman you are making or to the energy with which you are having difficulty. While chanting the divine name of the sphere, allow it to turn into its Queen scale color. See the sphere expand until it colors your entire aura.

Then, with this color permeating your whole body, concentrate on achieving the *positive* side of the astrological conjunction with which you are working. Someone with an afflicted Sun might have a problem with arrogance; an afflicted Scorpio Sun might be vindictive. During the exercise, the person with the afflicted Sun would be better off concentrating on leadership and self-confidence, while the person with the afflicted Scorpio Sun would be best off thinking about developing his or her spirituality.

Next, perform a complete Middle Pillar again to provide some balance. In the short term, this exercise should enable the energy to flow positively enough to perform a talisman ritual. In the long term, it will help prevent the energy from manifesting in a negative way.

Talisman Energy Machine

The techniques we have discussed require a magician to know himself or herself well enough to correct any imbalances. Often we have blocks that we are totally unaware of until we try to make a talisman that fails to work.

To solve this problem modern magicians have come up with a "machine" to measure energy levels in a talisman. Pat and Chris Zalewski, who use a pendulum to diagnose clients in their holistic healing practice in New Zealand, first suggested its use to me. Using the "machine," I have found that talismans that give low readings usually do not work, while those that give high readings are very successful.

The machine is a large piece of paper or cardboard on which a large circle has been drawn. The circle is halved, with the diameter running from nine o'clock to three o'clock.

The numbers one to ten are evenly divided between nine o'clock and three o'clock in the top semicircle, and negative numbers between –1 and –10 are placed in the bottom semicircle.

The talisman is placed in the center of the circle, and a pendulum is held above it with a relaxed hand. Say aloud, "What is the efficiency of this talisman?" After a while, the pendulum will start to move and then develop a definite swing toward one of the numbers in the dial.

If you were testing a banishing talisman, you would read the negative numbers; and for a positive one, you would read the positive numbers.

All talismans have a charge, but it is unlikely that it would be possible to make one that is totally charged.[1] Swings between zero and 100 (or –100 for a banishing talisman) can be safely ignored.

A well-made and consecrated talisman should register at about 80 to 90 (or –80 or –90 on a banishing talisman). This is a talisman that has attracted enough divine power to start making changes quickly and dramatically. A talisman that registers between 70 and 80 will work well, but its effects will be muted—it may take longer to bring about an effect. Talismans registering at between 50 and 60 are able to bring about changes, but their energy levels are so low that they are unable to stand out enough from the background noise of the universe. They will be too easily countered by the negative thoughts of the person for whom you made the talisman.

Personally, I would not bother keeping a talisman that registers at less than 70.

Low-yield talismans are not the end of the world. They can be fixed, but it is important to find out what went wrong, and the "machine" can help.

Setting up the machine as before, take a pencil in your left hand and point to each divine name. Ask the question, "What is the efficiency of this divine name on this talisman?" Do this for each of the names on the talisman, the intention, and the planetary seal. You will get a series of numbers; some will be higher than others. Usually, with low-yield talismans, there is one name that registers below 40 or 50, and that is the one you should be working on.

If it is a divine name of God that failed to have enough energy, you have to ask yourself some serious questions about the ritual's intention. It is possible that the talisman has failed to get the backing of the Divine and therefore should be abandoned. When this happens, you will usually find that your intention has a lower reading, too.

Another possibility is that there is an element of your personality that cannot handle this aspect of divine power. Unfortunately, there is no "patch" for this problem—you have to work it out yourself.

Meditate on the divine name, pleading that its secrets shall be made clear to you. Chant the name like a mantra until you feel the presence of the name about you like a cloak. Then just be still and wait for that aspect of Deity to unfold itself to you. After a period of days, weeks, months, or even years, you will have a realization about your relationship to that aspect of God, and changes in your life will follow. Until you make these realizations, it will be impossible for you to make high-yield talismans of this type.

If an angelic name fails to attract a high reading, it is best to visit the planetary inner temple and ask them why. If it is an archangelic name, it is possible that the talisman has failed to attract backing because it was not the right time for you to have your wish.

Say, for example, you made a talisman to prevent a person from bullying someone at work. If it worked properly, the bully would be prevented from attacking the victim completely; the bully would be sacked, promoted, or otherwise moved away from the victim. However, it might be more important for the victim to make a stand against the bully. Such stands are vital from the perspective of personal destiny. Once that stand is made, a talisman can be safely made to remove the bully from the person's sphere of influence.

Planetary intelligences have less spiritual reasons for refusing their help. Often it is because there is an astrological problem; either the planet was weak at the time of the consecration or the talisman's manufacture did not reflect planetary energy correctly (you may have painted it the wrong color or used the wrong planetary seal).

It is a good idea to use a computer to draw up a natal chart for the talisman as if it were a newborn baby born on the day of its consecration. The planetary power should be astrologically free to manifest and not be blocked by any squares or oppositions. For example, if you have made a solar talisman, the Sun should be in the best position possible and free from oppositions. This should be done before the talisman is manufactured as this will save you time having to glean the information from the planetary intelligence afterward.

Another reason why a planetary intelligence may not be able to give full backing for a talisman is because the planet was in a bad position in the magician's chart at the time of the ritual. Wait until the bad planetary aspect has passed from your chart and reconsecrate the talisman.

If a spirit name is causing problems, you should approach the planetary intelligence for more information. Do not approach the spirit directly, as spirits tend to be a little erratic. Sometimes they literally require an astral kick up the bottom to work correctly, and it is up to the intelligence to do that.

If an intention is giving a low yield, then check the letters in the mystical alphabet that you used to see if you wrote them correctly. Failing that, your intention may be poorly worded, confusing, or too elaborate. Generally, it is best to keep them simple. Another reason for a low yield is that the intention you wrote was not what you really wanted or meant to happen. I know of one man who made a talisman because he wanted wealth. He then bought a series of lottery tickets, but none of them came up. Disappointed, he tested his talisman and found that the intention only had a rating of 40.

Wealth talismans work to provide money and they are not that specific about how the wealth is generated (usually it is through hard work). When asked, the man said he always intended the talisman to attract money quickly through gambling. He rewrote the intention to make it earn money through gambling and consecrated another talisman. The intention rating shot up to 90, but unfortunately the Divine name and the archangelic name ratings plummeted, indicating that the universe was no longer interested in backing a talisman that required the man to make no effort for himself.

A failure in the planetary seal is usually caused by either it or the magic square being incorrectly drawn. If this is not the case, performing the consecration ritual incorrectly usually causes the problem.

You can find out if there is a fault with the consecration ritual by asking the "machine" to tell you how successful the ritual was. If you receive a number that is below 50, then you will have to perform the consecration ritual again. Sometimes the angels will tell you to do this anyway.

If all these tests prove positive it can be assumed that you have a weakness in dealing with this particular planetary energy. You should deal with it before you attempt to make another talisman with an intention of this kind.

Once a problem has been identified and resolved, consult the table below to see what action you should take. Sometimes you will be able to patch the talisman using the ritual given below. Always take the worst-case scenario when consulting this table. For example, if a planetary intelligence tells you that its name did not have a correct charge because of planetary alignments, you will have to perform the consecration ritual again—you won't be able to just repatch the ritual. If there are multiple problems identified, always choose the most drastic cure (usually this will mean destroying the talisman and starting again). Sometimes it will be necessary to destroy the talisman and build another, and other times it will be possible to use the ritual patch given below.

Table 22
Fixing a faulty talisman.

Talisman's fault	Action that should be taken
Divine name	Destroy talisman and create a new one.
Archangelic name	Use ritual patch.
Angelic name	Use ritual patch.
Intelligence name	Use ritual patch.
Spirit name	Use ritual patch.
Planetary seal	Destroy talisman and consecrate a new one.
Two or more divine or archangel names	Destroy talisman and consecrate a new one.
Intention	Destroy talisman and consecrate a new one.
Faulty ritual	Perform consecration ritual again.
Planetary alignments	Perform consecration ritual again.

Patching Ceremony

Perform a Banishing Ritual of the Pentagram and place the talisman in the triangle of the art and activate it. Consecrate the talisman with incense and water. Say to the divine name of the planet:

O thou who art (insert divine name), send forth thy current of power to inflame this creature talisman.

Visualize the King scale color of the sphere on the Tree of Life flooding the triangle of the art. Then call the name of the archangel, angel, intelligence, or spirit that has been inefficient.

O thou who art (insert name of being), send forth thy current of power to inflame this creature of talisman with thy name.

With the wand, draw the sigil of the creature above the talisman. See the light change to the appropriate Queen, Emperor, or Empress scale color. (Remember that if it is an archangel, it should be the Queen scale; an angel or intelligence, the Emperor scale; and a spirit, the Empress scale.) Visualize the being appearing in the triangle of the art as clearly as possible.

O thou who art (insert name of being), dwell within and work through this talisman to (read your intention).

See a ray of light come from the being into the talisman. See the energy light up the being's name and see the talisman burst into color. Raise your wand and say:

Thanks to thee (insert name of creature) for thy work this day. May there be peace between us.

Close the triangle of the art and perform a Banishing Ritual of the Pentagram and Hexagram.

Retest the talisman. If it has reduced in power or the patch has not improved the performance of the fault, then destroy it. It is clearly not meant to work.

How Should a Talisman Be Stored?

There is a school of thought that says a talisman should be carried about the person for whom it was made. The logic behind this is that the talisman's energy has the ability to assess directly the aura of the target with its energy. There are all sorts of wonderful stories about the efforts that magicians have used to try to get their enemies within range of their talismans.

One trick was to put a talisman in the victim's well so that whenever the victim drank from it, the water would be tinged with the talisman's energy. Sometimes they were placed in the thatch of a roofs or behind a chimney. There is one case of a love talisman being placed behind a mirror so that the person was exposed to it when she put on her makeup.

In actual fact, few talismans need to be attached to the target of their working. This is because they do most of their work on the astral plane, which is unaffected by time and distance; however, there are some that should be placed close to the person for whom it is made. Healing and personality improvement talismans should be placed either under the person's pillow or between the mattress and the bed frame. This enables the talisman to work directly on the person's aura and energy center's while the person sleeps. These talismans can do this without being in close proximity to the person, but somehow it is more efficient.

Travel talismans should be carried or placed in the person's suitcase. This is because problems that occur during traveling tend to be localized materially around the person, and the talisman can neutralize these quicker if it is close at hand. One person who kept his travel talisman in his suitcase found both missing when his plane landed. Baggage handlers had stolen the suitcase, but it was recovered by accident during a police check for illegal immigrants on a truck near the airport. The suitcase was returned within a day or so.

One could argue that if the talisman had been working properly, the suitcase would not have been stolen at all; however, the talisman's intention was to protect the traveler from harm. Any "attack" on the traveler's possessions was neutralized by the return of his property undamaged and the thieves being caught.

With some talismans, it is psychologically helpful to carry them, although technically it is not important. For example, you could take job talismans into any job interview, or carry knowledge, good luck, or memory talismans into exams. Protection or courage talismans are also good to carry.

Talismans that do not fit into the categories above should be stored safely in an envelope or box where they cannot be damaged. Do not put them in a lead or glass container or one that is lined with silk or rubber. These insulate the talisman's energy so that it is restricted to manifesting on the astral levels, which will slow its results.

Talismans should not be placed within ten feet of each other, as there seems to be some cross contamination between them. Neither should they be placed next to a strong electrical energy source, which distorts their energy.

Chic Cicero suggested a very good idea for storage that fits into the Cabbalistic symbolism of the talismans described in this book. Take a wooden box large enough to hold your talisman. Paint the inside and lower part black. Then, with acrylic paints, paint the lid in the colors of the sphere on the Tree of Life, Malkuth, in the Queen scale, i.e., citrine, russet, olive, and black. Then varnish the box.

A simpler version can be made out of two pieces of round, thick cardboard. One piece should be black, with the other piece painted in the colors of Malkuth. Place the talisman between the two sheets, with the black paint on the bottom like a sandwich filling, and sealed using staples or tape.

The effect of this symbolism is to place the talisman in the heart of the kingdom of results, which is one of the meanings of Malkuth. Obviously, a box or cardboard sandwich should not contain more than one talisman.

Making Talismans for Other People

Making talismans for other people enters you into an ethical nightmare. While it is acceptable for you to make talismans to improve your own lot, once you start making them for others it is vital to tread with care.

The number of "lessons" that are learned by making talismans or exercising magical power is astronomical. These lessons include the universe giving us what we actually ask for, the fruits of victory swiftly turning into ashes in one's mouth, to quote John Kennedy out of context.

If these lessons are ones that are hard learned for a magician who accepts that this is the way to learn, they will be that much harder for those who do not have enough magical training or ability to make a talisman of their own.

On the face of it, a magician should want everyone to be happy and get his or her heart's desire; however, if it is hard to know your own self truly, it is impossible to know what is best for others.

The main problem is that by the time people go to a friendly magician to sort out problems, they are usually at the end of their rope and think they have tried everything to solve their problems. The magician who offers to wave their worries away with a magic wand will appear to them to be offering a quick fix, something that will often not require them to do anything, or to even think about the mess they are in. Most of the time, the problems they have created are bought about by their own actions that they are unwilling to acknowledge.

Even healing, which many occultists distribute without question, requires a great deal of thought. Many illnesses are a device used by the universe to force people to wake up to things. Some people are shaken out of a stressful lifestyle by a sudden illness that gives them a warning.

There is a New Age trend to attribute some illnesses to negative thinking. For example, heart problems are caused by blocked emotions. Other long-term illnesses are symptoms of greater emotional and psychological problems. Cancer, for example, is caused by a self-destructive urge to kill oneself.

Like many New Age concepts, this is an oversimplification of a principle that is essentially correct. Disease is a symptom of a problem within the person, but that cause is as complex as an individual's psyche. It is superficial and lacking in compassion to say that anyone suffering from heart problems is an emotional cripple, or that cancer patients are victims of their own vices. It is also superficial to assume that because someone has realized the essential problem that caused his or her illness, that that person is going to be made well again. It may be that a particular realization was that person'e life's work, and the ability to face death afterward is his or her final victory.

So, what should a magician do, particularly as the magical brotherhood, the Rosicrucians, who are the template for many magicians, swore to heal everyone who asked? It is hard to think that you should not make healing talismans for others (or for yourself, for that matter), particularly when they are suffering so much. The way around this problem is in the intention you place on your talisman.

A healing talisman should not say, "May X be healed from illness." It would be better to say, "May the causes of X's illness be swiftly made plain and as a result may X be quickly healed in accordance to the divine will."

In such an intention, you have left the pathway of healing as a contract between Deity and the individual. In other words, you have focused on the individual rather than the illness.

Always target the person, not the result. Once the individual is better, then the result will happen. Do not make a love talisman so that someone can get a particular individual—make one that will help the person be more loveable and thus attract love in his or her life. Don't make a talisman to get someone through an exam—build one that will help them study, and so on.

This advice applies to making talismans for yourself, too. Don't think that you can hope to build a successful talisman that does not involve having to do some work yourself.

Once you have made a talisman for another, you should ask that person for an object in return. Traditionally, this is a coin of nominal value and its function is symbolic. It is basically a transfer of power between you and the person for whom the talisman was made. It enables you to transfer the link between you and your creation to the other person.

The coin should be handed over at the same time that you give the person the talisman. When done, you should visualize a silver chain extending from your heart center to the talisman. When the coin is handed over, you should see this chain disconnect itself from you and transfer to the other person's heart.

How Many Talismans Should You Create?

There once was a belief that a magician should only ever one talisman working at a time. Over the years this has changed as magicians made many talismans without any ill effects. I believe, however, that exposure to more than two talismans does confuse the person's aura. The person's unconscious needs time to digest the talisman's energy to bring about the desired result. Two talismans double the workload and will slow up the eventual results.

This does not affect the numbers of talismans a magician can create for others (although you should only make two for each person).

One word of warning: Every time you make and consecrate a talisman, you are bringing those energies and powers through you. For a time after every consecration, you might feel that you are exhibiting some of the virtues and vices of each planet. Generally, the only way around this is daily use of the Middle Pillar exercise and the

Cabbalistic Cross. I am warning you, though, that creating a talisman should not be done lightly and in the belief that it will not affect your life.

Destroying a Talisman

If a talisman has failed to work or if its job has been completed, it must be ceremonially destroyed and the entities that have been working to make your intention happen freed to do other work.

There are many different beings involved in the life of a talisman. Some beings, like those whose names you have called, you are aware of; but there are countless other entities, like elementals who are involved in making the intention come about but with whom you do not have direct contact. By their service to you, such creatures develop and evolve. It is therefore particularly important that they are released so that they can move on to the next stage of their evolution.

Destroying a talisman requires a simple ritual which should be performed whether the talisman worked or not. This is a demonstration of good manners to the beings who worked with you.

Rite of Ending

Place the talisman on the altar and light a single candle in front of it. On the South side there should be incense burning, and on the North side, consecrated water. On the West side of the altar, you should place a flameproof dish. Perform a Banishing Ritual of the Pentagram. Then speak to the talisman:

> *Creature of talismans, your work on this plane is performed, your life's work is complete. Therefore in the name of (insert divine name), I command you to cease your labors and meditate on your life's work before your transition.*

I would suggest that you leave the talisman before the candle for an hour before returning. This gives the entities within the talisman to contemplate their work, which makes their transition easier. Stand before the talisman and say:

> *Creature of talismans, may the blessing of the Crown of Crowns descend upon you for the work that you have done on my behalf. May there be peace between us for now unto the end of the ages. Now I prepare thee for thy journey.*

Purify and consecrate the talisman for the last time. Then, holding it in your hands, say:

> *Creature of talismans, in the name of (insert divine name), I free you from this mortal body. Quit this mortal frame and return to your own kingdom. Step into the light to see archangel (insert archangel's name) welcome you home.*

Put the talisman into the flame. Place it on the flameproof dish until it is thoroughly burnt, and then say:

> *It is finished.*

Perform a Banishing Ritual of the Pentagram and Hexagram. Take the ashes and bury them.

Destroying Other Kinds of Talismans

Large wooden disks and metal or clay talismans require a different sort of ending because they are harder to destroy. The destruction ritual is the same, except after the "step into the light" speech, you visualize a ball rising up from the talisman and stepping into the candle flame. Then take the talisman and cast it into a river or the ocean (if it will sink) or bury it deep in the earth.[2] Water will naturally disperse any latent power that remains in the talisman over a couple of week's time. Burial in earth takes about six weeks to remove any energy.

Some people want to keep talismans because of their artistic merit. I would be reluctant to do this because you can never be certain how persistent some beings are about clinging on to material bodies. If you want to do this, however, wrap the talisman in plastic and bury it for at least three months. Take the talisman out of the plastic. Perform a Banishing Ritual of the Pentagram through it (as I have described in the consecration of water rite) and let it soak overnight in consecrated water.

Use the talisman machine to test the talisman's potency. If it is more than 30 (or −30 for a banishing talisman), then it is still partly charged and you will have to bury it again for another three months.[3]

Sometimes it is not possible to retrieve the talisman, particularly if it is in the hands of another person; however, since you created it, you have a magical link that enables you to destroy it at a distance.

Simply visualize the talisman as clearly as possible and remember the words of the intention (ideally this should have been written down in your magical diary). Before the ritual, visualize the talisman on the altar and recite the intention several times. Then perform the ritual as normal, but burn the talisman in your imagination. If the talisman is ever returned to you, then, since the object will have ceased to be working, it only remains for you to destroy it by burning or burying.

Signs Following

Some people find it difficult to work a pendulum correctly; fortunately, there is another method of testing whether or not you talisman is working. This is a system that was developed by Madeline Montalban and is based on a magical principle that is fairly easy to understand. When you work magic properly, you create more power than you can possibly use. It saturates your aura for a period of time and creates coincidences. If you had performed a Mercury working, for example, you could find yourself seeing Mercury symbols or surprise gifts of orange flowers could be delivered. In one case, a company changed its corporate logo to orange.

These are called "signs following," and, in their own right, these prove that the magician has plugged into the magical energy enough to indicate that the talisman is working.

Montalban took the system a lot further. She said that a magician or witch should request from the archangel responsible for the talisman to give an indication that the request would be granted. She developed a list of prearranged signals that the archangels would give to show their consent. They were based on symbols and associations for each archangel. Some were quiet obscure and downright bizarre—like an attribution of blue budgerigars (parakeets of Australia) to Haniel, for example. Some of these prearranged symbols required an angelic miracle that was often even greater than the talisman's intention (the likelihood of you bumping into a member of a royal family in the United States, which is a sign for Sachiel, must be considered remote).

Practitioners of the system do report, though, that such obscure signs following do happen, usually closely followed by the talisman's intention coming to fruition. They define two different classes of signs. Second-class signs are those that are not one of the "official" signs, but are obviously connected to your working. One of these lesser signs could include someone sending you a postcard with a picture of the angel that you have invoked. There are usually about a dozen of these sorts of signs.

Then there are the "official" signs. Receiving at least one of them would confirm that the angel is working to bring about what you want.

I do not propose to reprint Montalban's official list;[4] however, over the last few years I have developed a list of my own that has been wired into this system of talismanic magic. To activate it, I suggest asking the archangel associated with the talisman on the Tree of Life to send you proof that the talisman is working correctly, using one of the symbols listed below, within seven days. This is best done immediately after the consecration of the talisman, before you close the temple. Otherwise, you can visit the planetary inner temple within twenty-four hours of making the talisman and ask for the archangel associated with it for one of the signs following.

I am opting for the Cabbalistic archangels of the Tree of Life instead of the planetary archangels. This is because the Tree of Life archangels are much less specialized and have more experience with human nature.

These signs have to be seen by you or by the person for whom you made the talisman. They have to be unexpected and connected with you and your life. Say, for example, that you have made a healing (Sun) talisman and as you drive along, you see a hawk. If you have driven along that road and seen a hawk before, it would not be considered a sign following; but if you have never seen a hawk along that stretch of road before, then it would be considered a sign following. Likewise, if after making a Saturn talisman you were contacted by your aged father, it would only be a sign following if you did not hear from him that often.

Table 23
Signs following.

Archangel	Sign that the talisman is working
Tzaphqiel (Saturn)	You receive a surprise call from an old man; an old woman who has no children; a skeleton; a funeral cortege; a raven; an elderly teacher; a scythe; black clothing; and lead objects.
Tzaphqiel (Jupiter)	Lightning storm; finding money on the street or a foreign coin in your change; a pay increase; an inheritance; purple clothing; a wheel; an emblem of royalty; and tin objects.
Camael	Sharp objects; surgery; cutting yourself; a red spot; fires; sparks; red lights (not traffic lights); a ram; a suit of armor; guns; military personnel; and iron objects.
Raphael	Birds; yellow flowers; a doctor; a golden sunrise; a sudden cure; a hawk; and gold objects.
Haniel	Doves; roses; a pregnancy; a birth; seven lamps; a ring; Cyprus trees; Cyprus; sea foam; and brass and copper objects.
Michael	Dragons; red crosses; newspapers; an old-fashioned pen; thermometers; cats; telecommunications; receiving news of an old friend; and rainbow-colored objects.
Gabriel	Dogs; shellfish; pears; spiders; moths; the sea; moonbeams; and silver objects.

---

1. Talismans that have not been consecrated carry a 10–20 charge simply because of the divine names and sigils that are placed upon them. Talismans made out of appropriate materials at the correct time sometimes carry charges of up to 50. Because 50 is enough of a reading to gain an effect, it explains why for a long time people did not consider it necessary to consecrate talismans.

2. Do not put it in a potted plant or window box.

3. Sometimes the pendulum will not move. This indicates a zero charge and the talisman is safe.

4. This has already been done in David Goddard's book *The Sacred Magic of the Angels* (York Beach, ME: Weiser, 1996).

Appendix: Banishing Rituals

Banishing Ritual of the Pentagram

In the air toward the East, draw a pentagram as shown in figure 61:

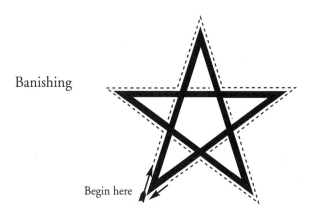

Banishing

Begin here

Figure 61. Banishing pentagram.

Bring your finger to the pentagram's center and vibrate the name YOD HE VAU HE. Imagine that your voice carries forward to the East of the universe.

Holding your finger out before you, go to the South, draw the pentagram, and vibrate the deity name ADONAI.

Go to the West, make the pentagram, and vibrate EHEIEH. Go to the North, make the pentagram, and vibrate AGLA.

Return to the East and complete your circle by bringing your fingers to the center of the first pentagram.

Stand with your arms outstretched in the form of a cross and say:

Before me, Raphael.
Behind me, Gabriel.
At my right hand, Michael.
At my left hand, Auriel.
Before me flames the pentagram.
Behind me shines the six-rayed star.

Again make the Cabbalistic Cross, saying ATEH, etc.

Banishing Ritual of the Hexagram

Perform the Cabbalistic Cross ritual. Facing East, draw the two triangles in figure 62 with your finger.

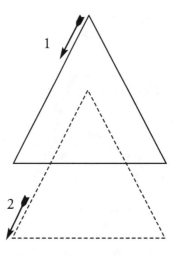

Figure 62. Eastern hexagram.

You should draw them from left to right and vibrate the name Ararita while holding your finger in the center of the two triangles.[1]

Next walk to the South with your finger outstretched. Draw the two triangles in figure 63, again vibrating the name Arirata.

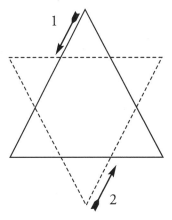

Figure 63. Southern hexagram.

Next walk to the West with your finger outstretched. Draw the two triangles in figure 64, again vibrating the name Arirata.

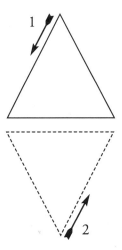

Figure 64. Western hexagram.

Next walk to the North with your finger outstretched. Draw the two triangles in figure 65, again vibrating the name Arirata.

With your fingers outstretched, return to the East to complete the circle, and then perform a Cabbalistic Cross.[2]

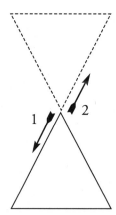

Figure 65. Northern hexagram.

Planetary Hexagrams

These are drawn above the talisman during the consecration ceremony (figure 66). Notice that there are six hexagrams that have to be drawn for a solar talisman (figure 67):

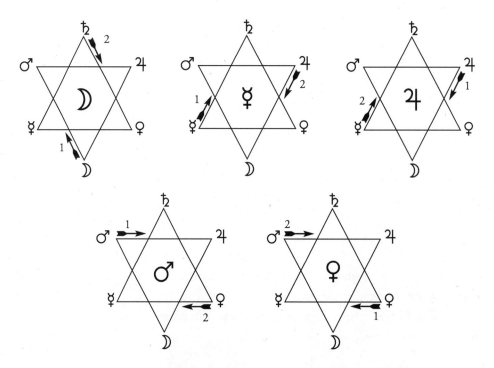

Figure 66. Planetary hexagrams.

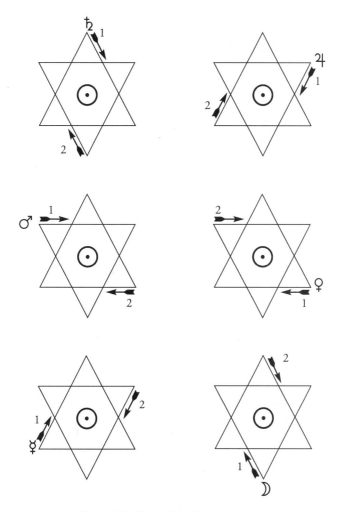

Figure 67. Six invoking hexagrams for Sol.

Setting the Seals:
A Neo-Pagan Replacement for the Banishing Ritual of the Pentagram

Stand in the East. Draw the symbol of your deity and see it glowing before you. Say:

By the power of the (state symbol) of (state deity), I seal the wards of the East.

With your figure extended, go to the South. Draw the symbol of your deity and see it glowing before you. Say:

By the power of the (state symbol) of (state deity), I seal the wards of the South.

With your figure extended, go to the West. Draw the symbol of your deity and see it glowing before you. Say:

By the power of the (state symbol) of (state deity), I seal the wards of the West.

With your figure extended, go to the North. Draw the symbol of your deity and see it glowing before you. Say:

By the power of the (state symbol) of (state deity), I seal the wards of the North.

Return to the East, finish the circle, and then stand in the center of the room. Visualize the four symbols at each quarter joined by a thread of blue light. Then say:

In this place of (state deity name), may the four winds be at peace. May earth, wind, fire, and water be harmoniously joined by the light of love.

Shout the deity's name three times and, as you do so, imagine diamond light extending from you heart center and filling the space you have created. Then say:

Let it be so.

---

1. Ararita is notarikon formed from Hebrew letters derived from the sentence "One is his beginning, One is his individuality, his permutation is One."

2. The Golden Dawn system required that a person carry out what was known as the *LVX formula* at this point; however, I believe that this is meaningless unless you have been initiated into the Inner Order of the Golden Dawn. The Cabbalistic Cross, if performed correctly, can achieve a similar effect for those who are outside the Order.

Bibliography

Agrippa, Henry Cornelius. *Three Books of Occult Philosophy.* Edited by Donald Tyson. Saint Paul, MN: Llewellyn Publishing, 1995.

Ashcroft-Nowicki, Dolores. *A Ritual Magic Workbook.* Wellingborough: Aquarian, 1986.

Budge, E. A. Wallis, trans. *The Book of the Dead.* New York, NY: Dover Publications, 1967.

Barrett, Francis. *The Magus.* York Beach, ME: Weiser, 2000.

Bohak, Gideon. "Aggressive Magic." The Michigan Society of Fellows and Department of Classical Studies, 1996 Exhibition. At the time of writing this book, the website address for this page was www.hti.umich/exhibit/magic.

Cavendish, Richard, ed. *Mythology.* Twickenham: Tiger, 1992.

Cicero, Chic and Sandra Tabatha. *Creating Magical Tools.* Saint Paul, MN: Llewellyn Publishing, 1999.

———. *Secrets of a Golden Dawn Temple.* Saint Paul, MN: Llewellyn Publishing, 1992.

———. *Self-Initiation into the Golden Dawn Tradition.* Saint Paul, MN: Llewellyn Publishing, 1998.

Cicero, Chic and Sandra Tabatha, eds. *The Golden Dawn Journal: Book 2 Qabalah: Theory and Magic.* Saint Paul, MN: Llewellyn Publishing, 1994.

———. *The Golden Dawn Journal: Divination.* Saint Paul, MN: Llewellyn Publishing, 1994.

———. *The Magical Pantheons.* Saint Paul, MN: Llewellyn Publishing, 1998.

Crowley, Aleister. *Magic in Theory and Practice.* New York, NY: Dover Publications, 1976.

Davidson, Gustav. *A Dictionary of Angels: Including the Fallen Angels.* Free Press, 1994.

Davies, Vivian and Renee Friedman. *Egypt.* London: British Museum Press, 1998.

Faulkner, R. O. *The Ancient Egyptian Pyramid Texts.* Oxford: Oxford University Press, 1969.

Fortune, Dion. *Cosmic Doctrine.* Wellingborough: Aquarian, 1988.

Gilbert, R. A. *The Golden Dawn Companion.* Wellingborough: Aquarian, 1986.

———. *The Golden Dawn Scrapbook.* York Beach, ME: Weiser, 1999.

Goddard, David. *The Sacred Magic of the Angels.* York Beach, ME: Weiser, 1996.

James, T. G. H. *Introduction to Ancient Egypt.* London: British Museum Press, 1979.

King, Francis. *The Flying Sorcerer.* Mandrake Press, 1986.

Knight, Gareth. *A Practical Guide to Cabbalistic Symbolism.* York Beach, ME: Weiser, 1969.

Kohnlenberger, John R. III, ed. *The Interlinear NIV Hebrew-English Old Testament.* Grand Rapids, MI: Zondervan, 1987.

Levi, Eliphas. *The History of Magic.* Translated by Arthur Edward Waite. Rider, 1913.

Martinez, David G. "PMich 757: A Greek Love Charm from Egypt," Ann Arbor, 1991. At the time of writing this book, this charm could be found in full at www.hti.umich/exhibit/magic.

Mathers, S. L. MacGregor. *The Book of the Sacred Magic of Abramelin the Mage.* 1897. Reprint. Chicago: The DeLaurance Company, 1936.

———. *The Key of Solomon the King.* 1888. Reprint. Translated by S. Liddell MacGregor Mathers. York Beach, ME: Weiser, 1986.

Matthews, John. *The Grail Seeker's Companion.* Wellingborough: Aquarian, 1984.

Regardie, Israel. *Ceremonial Magic.* Wellingborough: Aquarian, 1986.

Regardie, Israel, ed. *The Golden Dawn.* 6th edition. Saint Paul, MN: Llewellyn Publishing, 1990.

Schrire, T. *Hebrew Amulets.* London: Routledge & Kegan Paul, 1966.

Waite, Arthur Edward. *The Book of Ceremonial Magic.* Edinburgh: Wordsworth Reference, 1992.

Zalewski, Pat. *Evocations and Talismans in the Golden Dawn.* Thoth Publications, 2001.

———. *Z-5: Secret Teachings of the Golden Dawn, Book 1: The Neophyte Ritual 0 = 0.* Saint Paul, MN: Llewellyn Publishing, 1991.

Index